EGBERT STARR

MATCH

ISBN: 978-1-942839-03-3

Other titles available from Egbert Starr at most major on-line retailers, or visit egbertstarr.com

¡Arriviste! by Xerxes Melville de Felicio

Crucifying the Christ Within by Yonni Jackson

Trust by Fay Black

You Got What You Deserve by Bettina Lillemoore

Connect with Egbert Starr

Find on website: http://www.egbertstarr.com
Follow on Twitter: http://www.twitter.com/egbertstarr
Friend on Facebook: http://www.facebook.com/egbertstarr

Contents

MATCH

Introduction

In the middle of the divorce from my wife, I began a foray into Online Dating. After dancing my toe tips in the water for a few weeks, which meant not joining any service, which meant window shopping not buying, which meant fantasizing but no frakking, I plunged in headfirst and joined Match.com on the discounted six-month plan.

Not long into my online dating experience, ruing the difficulty at first of evoking responses from women, in spite of the care and attention put into my notes of interest, which were generated from my having taken a close look at their online written profiles, drunk them in, and felt an answer to, I realized that, as a writer, I was in a bizarre sort of quandary: I myself could not always distinguish myself between who I actually was, and who I was as a sort of fictionalized epistolary wooer. After all, I think every man who is seeking to either just have sex with a woman or genuinely seek her love and affection, is a distinct sort of self-made fiction anyway.

Increasingly, though, I became more and more successful at evoking written responses to my inquiries, leading, in turn, to more dates. But, though there is a wide array of writing styles and approaches in my letters, I wasn't a zelig; rather, the letters are an exploitation, an amplification of aspects of myself painted boldly, if not absurdly, to each woman I wrote and expressed my interest in. And this came about, primarily, by changes not so much in myself per se, but the vast differences of personality I was able to absorb by reading so many profiles and then, rightly or wrongly, respond to.

Quickly my letters of interest, answered and not, began to pile up. And very soon, I knew that, in addition to genuinely searching for someone to connect with, I was simultaneously writing a book. I became a sort romantic Lawnmower Man of myself, a man whose cyberworld of hopefuls became in the next instant played out in the real-life world of actuals. No sooner would I develop an online correspondence with a woman, than I was sitting across a Manhattan restaurant table with her; buying a chocolate bar two hours away for her; driving through the black hours of night to meet her in some strange New Jersey forest; or having sex with her in a faraway, tony suburb. The work was constant; I pored through thousands of profiles, read them all, and crafted letters to the several hundred I felt an internal click with, positive or negative.

My adventures from my home in upstate New York, took me to White Plains, Mamaroneck, Nyack, Beacon; several towns in New Jersey, and many times to Manhattan. I developed early on a very thorough system of saving and organizing my files, knowing that at a later date, without a system in place, I would be wading through an essentially indecipherable morass, and the project would be all but shot. As it was, for all my attention to detail, the book, for the hundreds of women I did write, was still a mess to put together.

In the midst of it, I had no idea how much and how many women I wrote. Between dating, and the hours spent driving, I read and wrote four to twelve hours every day. I did this in addition to my demanding full-time day job. When I was done, the 90,000 words of text, the equivalent of a full length novel, was a shock, but a good one. The fifteen stories also included, which divide the book into fifteen chapters, are recountings of dates I went on in their chronological order. Each chapter is named after a woman I dated, the story of whom concludes that chapter, preceded immediately by any initial correspondence between us. Each chapter also includes the bulk of initial emails I sent to other women I also sought to engage between these dates. All the dates, like all the letters, are nonfiction, which is the strangest thing about it all.

I realized, upon assembling the whole project and being able to view it as an entire work, rather than a disconnected collection of hundreds of emails, I had written a sort of six month spiritual autobiography — or just a really long love letter to myself. Only when it was finished could I see that there were patterns, both literary and psychological, that developed as a continuum in the chronology of these letters. While in the particular they may seem quirky or anomalous, the recurring allusions to Tolstoy's lovelorn aristocrat Levin from Anna Karenina, for instance, or swipes against Greenwich, Connecticut, where I grew up — these reveal, from a heart that begins the project pretty smashed over, a clear and steady path of healing.

Egbert Starr

Egbert's Online Profile

Playful, creative, and smart, I live a joyful life. This is true in my daytime work in the public sector, and in my work outside that time as a writer. I see myself as very fortunate in that I am able to use my own privileged background in both the direct service to others, which I love, as well as in the creation of art, which I love even more. Because of conscious choices I have made, rather than my constantly reaching for the latest gadget or gismo, though I have all the basic trappings of modern life, my relatively modest lifestyle provides me the greatest luxuries of all: time and solitude. These, I think, allow me to be as alert, as receptive, as restful, as aware, as focused, and also as supportive as I can possibly be. As a consequence, very little of my energies are drawn away to the margins; I do not lead a "busy" life; rather, I live a free one.

CHAPTER ONE: Mandy ("Motherleave")

LETTERS:

Hi, Hiro37

Dear Blackeye40

Dear Yalie40

Hi, Flywme2venus

Dear Hiddentreasure123

Dear Elle14

Hi Aryan12345

Dear Viaferry67

Dear Mallardlover35

Dear Motherleave [1]

Dear Motherleave [2]

STORY: Mandy ("Motherleave")

Hi, Hiro37,

You sound smart and open. As a photographer, it might be a good day to take pictures of New York — without people. Do you know the work of André Kertész? I love his pictures of New York, especially of water towers from the rooftops.

Where I am it's mostly snow, hills, and (right now) snow-covered trees. A different sort of photography.

I remember being in Vienna years back over Christmas. I was by myself. It felt like a cold, marble, ghost town. It made me feel special. I roamed past a small monument or grave even of Mozart's, and had a soda later at the bar where, I was told, Falco drank.

Egbert

Dear Blackeye40,

I confess: I'm a terrible pool player. But, I'm willing to become better.

Egbert

Dear Yalie40,

I like that you're "poised, prim, and proper"; but not only that, but that you know it, recognize it, and embrace it. I also like that you recognize that there is this other part of you that really wants to break free. Years and years ago, when I was blowing my mind away in Amsterdam, I realized very quickly that I had to get out of there fast. There was too much of the prim and proper in me, too much Ivy League etiquette, too much propriety to stay, I felt, without my very quickly losing control of virtually everything. So, I left. It is hard to keep the balance, hard to exist without tipping too much to one side or the other: too stiff and formal and rigid, going one way; or just a supernova human casualty blown away in space, on the other.

Best,

Egbert

Hi, Flywme2venus:

If, as you wrote in your profile, you've just read *Anna Karenina*, think about Levin. If you wanted to find one fictional character I most resemble, that's the one. For my money, the best passage in the whole book is when Levin is drinking *kvas* with the *muzhiks*. I love how Levin, in spite of the jeers of the peasants, works in the fields until he gets the swing of harvesting right. Later, of course, this intellectual, Trust Fund aristocrat, is accepted as a fellow among men.

If I am as you put it "mesmerizing to your eyes," then perhaps you'll plunk down twenty-odd bucks and reactivate your account, instead of just collecting and dumping a lot of electronic junk mail from non-artistic guys without much more than an idle, ongoing heartbeat who tumble by cybersphere like spaceweeds, and who on occasion, bump against the side of your bed and whom you, just as swiftly, like summer flies, brush away.

Egbert

Dear Hiddentreasure123:

You write, "Work like you don't need money, Love like you've never been hurt."

Not a bad motto. It's hardly unusual, however, that these two things, Love & Money, are paired together. While I'm no astrological guru, I do know that they are paired in the same house of the zodiac, like tobacco & candy in the drugstore (see [or Google] Plato's *pharmakon*). You do make an allusion to your having been badly hurt through love in the past; I feel that deeply in your profile. Yet, in spite of your sorrow, grief, and pain, I also feel your heart's never smothered yearning. I'm going to guess that you have compensated through financial success to offset those other losses. Somehow, the house of ourselves always has to stand. And, for whatever else you might dismiss about Freud, one nail I think he hit the head of truth on was that human happiness involves having the magic pair of Love & Work.

You're not so hidden. It seems like you're a true beauty who's beginning to her open heart to the world again.

Egbert

Dear Elle14,

I drifted, without subscribing, to a number of different sites over the past few weeks, and there are certainly other sites that are much more meat-markety than this one; there are others, too, such as Chemistry.com (the sister site to Match), that make themselves out to be quite scientific, if not merely methodological.

I'm going to assume that your plea about treading with caution is directed toward (or against) men reading your profile kindly being asked by you to look elsewhere if they're not looking for anything more than the proverbial good time, not for them to be careful that all you're looking for is that, and if they want more, they're going to get their little boys' hearts broken!

It is bizarre, as you say, that something genuinely good could come of this — that out of nothing, could come something. In a weird way, it's actually upliftingly human, because it is, in the end, so, well, not scientific. And if it's a cute and civilized meat market, it's not a market just for the body, but, I think, for the mind and spirit, too. And that, I think, is what we are all shopping around here on this site mostly for.

Egbert

Hi Aryan12345:

While my garden is buried in snow right now, I grow arugula by the bushel, and make a great salad. I live farther away than you say in your profile you want to toss your stones, but who knows, maybe it could turn into an adventure.

I hope to hear back from you.

Egbert

Dear Viaferry67,

You proposed that I ask you some questions to know more about you; so, here goes:

If you like art, would meet me at the Met and look at the Baker Dancer?

Do you ski? Are you any good, if so?

Do you like guys who are brilliant, over the top brilliant?

Are you an inventive person? A right-brainer? Left-brainer?

Do you fall in love? Have you felt your heart break?

Do you laugh when you read Plato?

Are you in love with Glenn Gould?

Does it make you sad that Kurt Cobain killed himself?

Flaubert says to live like a bourgeois and think like a madman. What's your response to that?

Egbert

Dear Mallardlover35,

Yes, you are very smart and very funny. But who doesn't at least try to lead with his or her best shoe first? To a certain extent, I look at this as a cheap place, as in inexpensive, where bunches of my own little demons come up, little geists and whatnot, momentary evocations of longings and sudden intimations. And truly, for each letter I write that hardly ever gets written back to, a part of me does come alive. There are of course a lot of dolts out there, but so what? It's a little painful that smart and aware people, and I'm one of them and so are you, will never find the big thing, as you put it here, but so what, too. Your blunt friendliness was a real nice kick in the pants to run across.

Egbert

Dear Motherleave,

You are a totally amazing person. Lines like, "I don't drink much but I like dirty bars," are brilliant. Pictures that toggle between something that looks like the Winter Palace and somewhere in the Third World, stunning. You actually take all your loose ends and throw them on this site as nobody else has done, and dare to show yourself to be unique. You are incandescent.

Egbert

Dear Motherleave,

I've looked at your words again. And your pictures.

You are a genius.

Egbert

Mandy ("Motherleave")

We got along great with each other; both of our intellects were on the perimeter, and our conversation was as easy as smashing endless glass bottles together with endless piles of rocks at hand. When Mandy sat on my bed, I knew it meant I had to sleep with her, that that was expected, that that was how things were done, that it would be inhospitable, rude, and would cause problems if I didn't.

It didn't feel like it was something I could, without causing a scene, given how well everything else had gone, avoid. So, we had sex. It felt like I was supposed to, that it would be better if I just did. So this, I thought to myself, is what it is like to be a girl. It was just easier for me to have the sex.

Before that, soon after I had written Mandy that night, we had messaged each other; and soon, too, she countered my suggestion for me to drive to Brooklyn, or at some point in between, for her, instead, to drive upstate. And, by 2 am, a small blond girl, an elfin one with narrowing eyes, was pulling into my driveway in her pickup truck from Red Hook with a stack of LP's under her arm to play on my tube amplified stereo.

Because the cat had knocked the tonearm off the turntable and broken its delicate harness from which it hung balanced almost weightlessly, the Leonard Cohen and the fistfuls of music she brought could not be played. Mandy tried to fix it, and I saw she could be of use like this, that she liked to fix delicately engineered things that were broken.

She was like a surgeon dealing with a heartwreck, but I didn't have the right tools, and it was hopeless for the night. She quit like it was over before it began, a switch in mood that was as sudden as her initial determination to fix it.

Next week I visited her. When I got off the F-train, she was waiting for me in her pickup truck, beaming. It was beautiful and romantic, and I felt beautiful to have a woman waiting for me, just as we had planned, to the minute. I began to be a little bit put off when she told me that her apartment's doormat that cheesily spelt out Robert Indiana's tilted LOVE-thing was a gift from her husband, from whom she had been separated for five years already; and her recent grief over a year-long relationship with another man who broke it off with her because his wife had become pregnant, was also alarming.

At the same time, even though she mispronounced a few words, such as a flat schwa in "undulate," the sign of an autodidact more than a poseur, her wall, which was a map pinning in place her eighteen months of world travels between Iraq, Russia, and India, where alone she had traveled to mourn the death of her father, when she was thirty-seven, drew me in.

I loved Mandy's voice, and had a hard time erasing it from my answering machine. It was polite and clear and confident — like a descendant of Katharine Hepburn's might be, if you imagined that. Having myself over twenty-five years ago been a sort of land rover, seafarer, I felt both jarred and at home to hear Mandy's far flung stories of being "fucked like a dog" by a Russian ship captain in the middle of the Black Sea; and later, when fearing for her safety from Moscow's underworld, how she stole his address book and fled his apartment; only to return, two months later from Istanbul to give the book back.

When she offered to show me her papers that she was clean from diseases and not to worry about getting her pregnant because she had had a ten-year, copper-plated IUD inserted, I was only half relieved.

The next time she came upstate, I returned home in the afternoon after work to find that Mandy, rather than having used the day to work on the book she was writing about her unresolved relationship with her deceased father, and for which I had invited her to spend the time doing, she had cleaned my house from top to bottom. It was spotless. "There were black hairs everywhere," she said. The correct assumption I let pass was that the hair Mandy had discovered had belonged to my ex-wife.

She wiped her brow; her hair was blond. She talked about how she had moved the bed. She talked about how she had turned the mattress over. She was fairy-like, five foot one; it was a king-sized mattress. She told me she had done my wash. I told her that the wicker basket that had been full of clothes that she had also washed had been clean clothes. She told me that she hadn't had time to fix the hinge on the refrigerator door that, because of how the door swung, was threatening the refrigerator's seal.

She called me "Dear" a lot, and at dinner began telling me about the recipe she had used tonight, and about other recipes she had gotten from her mother-in-law. Like the tiniest crack of light that gets in, she must have seen a flash of discomfort cross my face. She jumped up from the table and began clearing our dishes and washing them.

While the water from the sink was pouring from the faucet, she shouted at me to tell her what the fuck my problem was. I told Mandy that I would after she had calmed down and we both were seated again. Fifteen minutes later, the dishes drying on the wooden rack, I told Mandy that I'd prefer it if we didn't invite our ex's to dinner, that I just wanted to have dinner with her.

I barely remember any of her anger that came next when Mandy left in her truck. We did not go to the opera *Orphée et Eurydice* at the Met to which she had invited me and bought tickets for the next day ever.

CHAPTER TWO: Julianne ("Classact")

LETTERS:

Dear Emma1206

Dear Eeek

Dear Sparky1988

Hi, Eden347

Dear Lemongelato

Dear Opusturkey

Dear DJ747

Dear Lonelyplanet1

Dear Iheartsammy

Dear Madeinamerica

Hi Classact

STORY: Julianne ("Classact")

Dear Emma1206:

I really like your writing about "the twinge in the gut with certain people," which is why I'm writing you. The twinge, yes. Believe it or not, I've got the Sex Pistols live on vinyl, which I can play on a totally ear-crushing tube amplified stereo. Nonconformist? Ivy League? But usually, truth be told, these two seldom come in the same candy wrapper. But when they do, they can be absolutely great.

I can tell you've really got something. Few people ever put together twinkle and twinkle, as you have.

I hope you write back.

Egbert

Dear Eeek:

I'm not tall. But I am a quirky, smart, movie buff with a top-notch education, like you. You've been to the one place I've had in mind as a fantasy to go to for years: Iceland. A people, a language, and a location that haven't changed in over a thousand years.

I hope you write me back.

Egbert

Dear Sparky1988,

I hope I do not offend you, since you are after all a graduate of both Cornell and Columbia, by pointing out that you might consider changing the second "a" in your word "advanturous" to an "e." It'd make better copy, of course; and bring out the color of your eyes. I have also noticed just now that you claim to be a mixture of an introvert and an extrovert. In fact, your entire profile is a balancing act of steady complements. I see that better now; I suppose, while you seem a little pressed against the rail behind you in your photo, I was somewhat blinded by your salient attractiveness, if I may make so bold and declare. I have. An absolute beauty. Fortunately, you know your "own limits," and coming from someone in your field, that has a particularly significant weight. I would cherish herewith at some point in the future, if that point in time should ever come, to engage you in the opportunity to meet at the Cloisters to carry on a discussion about the missing Unicorn tapestry.

Egbert

Hi, Eden347:

You are funny and smart and right on the money all the way.

Believe me, most of these profiles sound like crap; mine included. Mine makes me sound like a mixture of Henry James and Yoda with normal word order. And that's bad. But, listen, I'm pitching to a different crowd. All their edges, smoothed off. Half of them worried about never having children. It's awful, really awful.

You sound like you are all right. Just don't fall for some jerk-off in overalls and a slide rule who thinks he's smarter than you. He probably won't be. And beware of phrases like "emotionally mature," and what was that other one you said, "goals" or "career," or something like that. These things have no meaning. A goal is a point scored in soccer. And a career is what people who have no life purpose pursue; it's about as generic as any commuter standing on any platform. Avoid at all cost. Please. The world needs people like you.

While you're too far away, and I'm way out of your age range, good luck.

Egbert

Dear Lemongelato:

I've been around folks with a little less education than you who guzzle wine, or "avidly," as you call it. And I've heard people hammer and hammer away at me with their monolithic diatribes, sometimes due to the old vino and sometimes not, and I have pretty much forsworn such "riveting" conversationalists. You do hit one nail smack on the head: "proactive" most certainly is a cover word for aggressive. Part of the problem, as I see it, is by people's using the catchwords and catchphrases of the day, in spite of their intentions to "say what they mean and do what they say," is that they don't really know and aren't really aware of what their words, metaphors, references, and phrases themselves mean themselves first off; and the result is that, unbeknownst to themselves, they do not say at all what they had meant or intended. Everything, as a result, looks like icing, but there really is no cake. One could pass an entire lifetime like this, and every friendship and love affair goes on like another conversation one might have had with strangers in an elevator.

That said, it is certainly hard to put oneself out there, to come up, in a handful of sentences, with something original and true. The sadness is that we are all on this site now broadcasting those clumsily put essences of a self we imagine to be ours which we of course wish others had noticed in us themselves. The magic is when another notices our inner magic and from that alone wants to know us more. That is the beginning of true romance, to be noticed, seen, heard like the bluebird sitting on a branch somewhere in the forest.

Egbert

Dear Opusturkey,

You look and sound quite polished, which might get you someplace on this site. But the more I pore through it, the more I get the sense that it's a shopping mall for people in finance or people who are sorry that they're not. People who get excited (and you might want to touch up that little typo [exited] on your profile) by ideas, I'm getting the sense are put off by anything close to one here. But do you really group books and politics and anything under the sun together? They are quite different, you know. I like talking about candy and Moroccan fezzes, if that's how it's spelt, and Sappho. See how these all stand apart? They really are different subjects altogether. And I do mean altogether, as in completely. But, again, there really is a sad warmth to your gaze which (I think I can pull it off rather than the plainer "that" here) befits the general style of your writing. Well, that about wraps up another missive popped into the mailbox without a stamp. Good luck in all your future endeavors.

Egbert

Dear DJ747:

I am getting the feeling that this site is altogether wrong for artists and thinkers. You are practically the first person I've run across who's not a banker making 150+. What a relief! You're actually DOING something with yourself and your life! I am highly educated, supersmart, nimble, and creative. See what this site has done to me? I'm spitting out laundry lists like the rest of 'em. Let me put it like this: Franz Kafka in his diary notes how he was reading Goethe's diary, and he notes how Goethe had an entry one day that said: Today, did nothing. Kafka's point was just how monumental that "doing nothing" was for a man like Goethe to actually write "did nothing." But everyone on this site I'm afraid would only say: What's so special about doing nothing? Why, because people who don't actually do stuff, do things, because they do so much of nothing on an ordinary daily basis, they can't identify with Goethe's noteworthy disaster of doing nothing, instead of creating.

I hope to hear back from you.

Egbert

Dear Lonelyplanet1,

Cheer up!

No need to be lonely. There are billions of people!

Egbert

Dear Iheartsammy:

You wrote, "But the point I am trying to make is that one of the essential goals of dating is to see if your perceived good qualities are viewed as such by someone else."

I'm in, I think, the second stage of this online dating ritual extravaganza. I already hate my profile because it makes me sound a lot stuffier than I am. I'm not stuffy, not until I'm pushed up against a wall, at any rate. Anyhow, your comment that I quoted above stopped me dead in my tracks. And, too, what will doom or drag out a relationship until the next Doomsday is the failure of the other (or both) people to see those good qualities. Few things are really more important in a relationship than being seen and being heard. Your comment, really, helped me. What I thought I'd do here on Match (stage one) is not pussyfoot around; look myself in my own mirror, and lay my cards on the table. I mean, if you don't know me, it's hard to accuse me of arrogance or even self-delusion if I confess to my being brilliant. Doesn't everybody want a brilliant girlfriend, boyfriend? In my world, yes.

Egbert

Dear Madeinamerica:

Your opening line is great.

Unfortunately, none of the ladies I've emailed practically has returned even a "No, thanks." I must not have that Playboy, Porn Addict, Pervert vibe that catches all the little flies. Your clarification of what goes on here has helped me out immensely.

Thanks,

Egbert

Hi Classact,

I'm supersmart, superfit, and superplayful. Like you, you can dress me up and dress me down.

Hope to hear back from you.

Egbert

Julianne ("Classact")

Julianne was open to meeting me for a cup of coffee, so she agreed to meet me for lunch at a midtown Moroccan restaurant that I'd picked by going online and searching for one. When I got in, I knew it was the wrong place and the wrong girl; I mean, I knew it was the girl I'd agreed to meet, but she looked nothing like her picture, and it had to be her because, besides me now, she was the only other customer in the dead restaurant.

Julianne was homely, her clothes were in terrible taste — her red knit dress had stitched into it some tacky designer label word like "Armand" in script over and over the entire thing; her hair was thin & the ends split; her skin was just terrible. All in all she just looked like an unhealthy human being who'd been eating too many potato sticks and other junk food out of cans and didn't know a thing about grooming herself.

Even these things I could have tolerated, or excused, but during our meal she picked her teeth behind the turned fingers of one hand to cover what she was doing in her mouth with the fingers of the other. During our meal she took four cell phone calls — three business and one personal. Julianne had, in short, a gross lack of grace and etiquette. It was systemic. She wasn't rude to the extent that sometimes what she said or did was off-color, or on occasion vulgar. She was, I hate saying this, altogether common.

It was for this that I could neither fault nor blame Julianne for anything. She made me feel, in contradistinction, my many privileges that I could see I take generally for granted; even if it makes me feel also a little bit guilty of feeling at times a bit snobbish, when, in fact, I really do not see myself as a snob at all.

I simply have had the good fortune to be well-educated, good-looking, well-groomed, and healthy. These are the corners of my many advantages, none of which Julianne herself in life appeared to possess. So, how could I fault her? She, like me, was just another person trying to make it the best way she could in this world.

Throughout our date, I was polite, good humored, and courteous. I asked Julianne questions, but did not probe. I talked a bit about my job, and Julianne said very little about hers, only that she worked nearby in finance. With the waitstaff, I was friendly, but not overly so. All in all, I was personal, but easy going.

It is easy for me to be this way, and I left on the table an appropriate and decent tip along with the check. Having exited the restaurant, whose food had been mediocre at a stretch, I walked Julianne to the nearest corner; she didn't thank me for taking her out. She didn't know to shake a hand.

In this world, I later realized, it is perfectly easy to behave like a gentleman before a beautiful, aware, intelligent, and joyous woman. Anyone can do that. It is easy. But a real gentleman knows how to be one and is one when the chips are down, and the person opposite him lacks all the graces and good fortune that somehow, through luck and birth and experience, he has had in life, and she, through no fault of her own, has not. A date is a date, lunch is lunch, and a commitment to have lunch with another human being for an hour is a commitment. It is kept. That is all.

CHAPTER THREE: SUZIE ("nonpareil")

LETTERS:

Hi, Iluvnycity

Dear Fairytale

Hi, Yukele582

Dear Sweetmaria

Dear Angeltune

Dear Grannyluv

Dear Homestaple

Dear Mendontrule

Dear Betabeauty

Dear nonpareil:

STORY: Suzie ("nonpareil")

Hi, Iluvnycity—

You know, this site is beginning to kill me. Everybody with a half a semester from Norwalk Community College to PhD's from Yale is equalized as having a good heart and being down-to-earth. You, I'm afraid don't appear anymore down-to-earth than [edit; substitute] a raging peacock does guarding the Pharaoh's wall. I mean you seem splendid: intelligent, fashionable, beautiful, etc., but down-to-earth? That's like a park bench that's been painted over the same color green a few times over twenty years. Down-to-earth, isn't that like an egg sandwich for $1.99 or $2.49 with cheese? Nobody in the upper echelon of academia and certainly working for a New York law firm can claim to be down-to-earth anymore, anymore than I can claim to be a humble peasant myself working for a few shillings in the peat. All this droning, overweening palaver is really beginning to make me nuts, loopy. Have you seen the take-out of Sacha Baron Cohen as Borat in the supermarket being shown the endless aisle of butters and cheeses repeatedly by the store manager, the multitudes of brands, styles, and varieties ad nauseam? "And what this?" he asks, dropping the copula as usual. "This," says the manager, who's got the patience of the Wedding Guest (but nobody knows what this is anymore because nobody is really educated anymore; they've got degrees, but they're ill-read: hence, not educated; trained, yes; educated, not) "is cheese." I'm afraid everything here just looks like cheese to me. And for all the talk about wanting "interesting" conversation, playfulness, and surprises, the first moment there is a mere hint of the real thing, you know, a thinking active playful inventive funny sardonic provocative mind, the screen door slams, the bolt flies in the lock, the mute button is pushed, the profile is deleted, the head turns away.

Egbert

Dear Fairytale:

I admit: I am frustrated. I wouldn't wink at someone online anymore than I'd so in public. Sure, there must be a dozen guys, excuse me, dozens of guys who claim they're creative and independent, write well, and think deeply. I know. But, tell me, is my profile so ornery, or what, that almost no one writes me back? Like next to zilch. Oh, right; I'm not in NYC. But it's not like we're getting a sonogram tomorrow, right?

OK. That was a little steam. Sorry to pick you, but my thumbnail updater says you're online right now, and you're the best chance of an actual reply. Obviously you're smart, literate, and attractive. And you're self-aware. All pluses. You mention East Berlin. Yes, I love it; or, shall I say loved it. It's been a while, I confess. When I went, I was hassled by Checkpoint Charlie himself in 1988. It was a very good year.

I hope to hear back from you. Seriously, I do.

Egbert

Hi, Yukele582,

I think you either spurned or dumped me before. I don't know why. You say in your profile's heading, "Let's try"; so, I did.

Egbert

Dear Sweetmaria,

For nearly a week now, I have held onto your profile without writing you, just to feel through what I had to say and not blunder. There is nothing at all "self-absorbed" in what you say, and you don't "rattle on" anywhere. There is, I feel, a deep core of calm self-understanding to you. You also strike me as a genuinely grateful person, in a big picture, life-seeing way. Experience, at the same time, has not left you bitter, resentful, angry, or jaded. Rather, it has only made you clearer, and your own articulate sense of your life-view more developed.

You recognize that it is not your job today to heal an injured man. It is his job. Healing and love are not the same; it seems as though you had to learn that. To love is a life-long responsibility; healing others, even when we choose to do so, as Mother Theresa did, we do so to heal ourselves. This, though, is not your life's mission. You will support the healthy man and love him forever no matter what. That is clear to me, and that is central to your life's mission. And you will do this with never-ending playfulness, lightness of being, and smiling devotion. Your own health will increase and you will become even happier and more radiant day by day with the loving kindness of a man who is healthy and who is equally devoted to you. That is the personal life you deserve.

So, it becomes incumbent upon me now to look myself in the mirror and ask myself could I be him to you? It is possible; I can feel that easily and clearly from the words you write. In addition to my ever-bountiful childlike essence, it is important that I acknowledge to myself and say to you that I am also a man who keeps in his stable a team of dark horses. People, you have learned, don't actually change each other. They may try, but they can't. People can change themselves or not. People, do, though, allow parts of themselves to come out. While simple and reductive, it's fair, I think, to see that a deeply good person will give off the feeling of safety that will allow for the depth of goodness in another to come out, too. That becomes a mutually loving and mutually healthy space to live in and grow in. But what about your blackened horses? Where are they? Do you know? In what forest, stable, land, or meadow are they still hidden?

Egbert

Dear Angeltune:

I am a genius.

You are young and hot.

You play guitar, an amateur.

I play piano, an amateur.

You're going to New Hampshire.

I'm staying in New York.

If you get involved with me, you will fall in love with me.

If I get involved with you, I will fall in love with you.

This will cause all sorts of hardship, heartbreak, stress, and longing.

You will get your MBA.

I will keep my MFA.

You will never forget me.

I will always remember you.

Egbert

Dear Grannyluv:

Good day, and how do you do? I read your profile with some interest, and feel tempted now to woo you in the only way that I know possible: by myself. If I had a friend, or several, to describe me in my first paragraph, this it what they would tell you about me: he is absolutely brilliant, a genius, hysterically funny, a most excellent listener, really quite splendid in areas where it counts big-time, and cute as a button. But, without them around to do my dirty work for me, I'll have to skip that portion of my courtship.

Now that I've put my ventriloquist back in his box, it's time for me to talk. You are lovely and beautiful, but how on earth can a man "woo" you in the old-fashioned (by the way, it's got an -ed on the end, like use to used to, too), when you've got the audacity to post two pictures of Johnny-come-latelies hanging on you like wallpaper? Seriously, you're far too attractive to present yourself to qualified gentlemen aspiring to wrap their arms around your pleasure domes like that. Any mom who knows what a pinch of salt is worth would tell you the same. Even if the dudes are your brothers, it's all what you project, honey. It's all in what you show them. And don't. Nobody's going to come 'round the corner and sweep you off your feet if your torso is held by another. Especially with that threatening shot of you kicking the guy in the groin. Ouch! That pic of you teeing off? I'm just gonna cover my fig leaf and close my eyes for the rest.

Egbert

Dear Homestaple,

Maybe you're just a model, or like one, a nice, fun person who just happens to be one of Nature's freaks of incredible beauty. If you don't like what my face looks like, no sweat. As you said: it's only Match.com. Good luck!

Egbert

Dear Mendontrule:

I am getting better at this. I'll see a face, a pair of eyes, read about a line-and-a-half, scroll down some, and say to myself: she's really, really smart. For you, it was where you say, "Yoga and the like." It was "the like" part that did it for me. Obviously. There's a brilliant, self-aware one, pal. So, it doesn't turn out to be a surprise where you or another went to school except the way Laurie Anderson might go, "Right. Again."

Me, I'm the swear dirty, Henry James type that nobody believes is a Jew until I give them my Bertrand Russell stare and tell them, "I'm too smart to be a Christian." Then, there's that "ensuing pause" as was noted in the 1787 record of the Philadelphia Convention. But what in G-d's good name do you mean with that "stipulate that that feeling is mutual"? Are we drawing up contracts about how we must feel? Or, more likely, a flare from your rowboat in Chesapeake Bay that a few captains have already lied and thrown you overboard, or that you've played el capitan yourself and chucked them into the great milchy waters of life's oblivion (hence your dominant/submissive paradigm).

Don't get me wrong. I think you're the cat's meow. Just say the word, and I'll meet you at the closest Stuckey's north of your home and south of mine. I'll be that genius-type fella holding up an Almond Log Roll near the checkout counter.

Egbert

Dear Betabeauty:

YOU SMOKE, DRINK, NEVER EXERCISE, BOAST OF BEING CRABBY 3/4 OF THE TIME AND WRITE IN CAPITAL LETTERS. WHY WOULD ANY FOOL, AS YOU WRITE, BE "SCARED OFF BY NOW"? WELL, BESIDES THE BILLBOARD-LIKE PRESENTATION, I GOT A KICK OUT OF YOUR PROFILE. YOU PRETTY MUCH ADMITTED WHAT WE ALL KNOW: WE ALL BUY TOILET PAPER, CLIP OUR NAILS ON OCCASION, AND GO TOO FAST THROUGH THE E-Z PASS LANE. YOU'RE LIKE THE IVORY SOAP GIRL WITH SMOKE IN HER LUNGS AND BOOZE IN HER VEINS. AS A RE-COVERED JUNKIE, I SPEND A LOT OF TIME AT THE GYM GETTING MY HIGH IN WHAT WE REFER TO AS A SOBER WAY, PUSHING MY ENDORPHIN LEVELS WAY UP TO NEAR LETHAL LEVELS ON THE ELLIPTI-CAL MACHINE, AND I SELDOM SEE WOMEN WHO ARE CLOSE TO HALF AS FIT AS YOU APPEAR TO BE. MAZEL TOV. HONESTLY, IF YOU DON'T MIND MY TOSSING IN A COUPLE OF PENNIES, YOU DON'T RE-ALLY NEED A MAN. SURE, I KNOW WHAT IT'S LIKE WITH THAT KING-SIZED BED I CAN SLEEP IN AT VIRTUALLY ANY ANGLE UNDISTURBED, NOT HAV-ING TO ENGAGE IN EARLY MORNING CHIT-CHAT ABOUT DEFROSTING BONELESS CHICKEN BREASTS FOR SEVEN MINUTES PER POUND WITH A LOVED ONE, AND IMAGINING THAT SPECIOUS FEELING OF INTIMACY WITH ANOTHER A VERY SMALL PERCENTAGE OF THE TIME, WHEN MOST OF IT IS SPENT KEEPING CLEAR OF EACH OTHER LIKE A CAT UNDERFOOT. WHY ON EARTH WOULD YOU OR ANYBODY WANT TO CHANGE THAT? LISTEN, I'M GOING TO LISTEN TO THE SAME LEONARD COHEN TRACK ON REPEAT FOR AS LONG AS IT PLEASES ME, FOR AS LONG AS THE MUSIC MAKES

ME HAPPY. THERE IS NOTHING WRONG WITH SELF-SATISFACTION. THINK OF ALL THE WONDER-FUL, FULFILLING, LIFE-GIVING THINGS YOU DO. YOU ARE NOT MERELY "BUSY" AS YOU DESCRIBED YOURSELF. "BUSY" PEOPLE ARE BUSY COUNTING PAPER CLIPS THEY'VE SPILLED ON THE FLOOR, MEASURING CUPS OF RICE, AND COUNTING CAL-ORIES LIKE IT'S A SACRED BIRTHRIGHT. YOU, ON THE OTHER HAND, ARE ENGAGED. LOOK AGAIN AT THAT PICTURE OF YOU WITH THAT VERY OLD WOMAN. SEE? THAT IS NOT BUSY. YOU'VE GOT A REALLY BEAUTIFUL AND REAL SMILE, AND, EXCEPT FOR THAT OMINOUS MAN-KILLING MANTA RAY IN THE PHOTO, YOU ARE THE KIND OF WOMAN MEN LIE THEIR PATHETIC ASSES OFF ABOUT DURING ENDLESS ROUNDS OF JOINT THERAPY OVER THAT THEY SAY THEY WANT TO BE WITH, INSTEAD OF THE DIMINUTIVE DORMOUSE THEY'VE HOOKED UP WITH FOR A DOZEN YEARS OR MORE AND CAN'T STAND BECAUSE BY NOW SHE'S ALL BUT CRUSHED AND LIFELESS, BUT DON'T HAVE THE GUTS TO BE TAKEN OUT TO DINNER BY. IN MY BOOK, YOU ARE ALREADY ONE OF LIFE'S GREAT WINNERS.

Egbert

Dear nonpareil:

You and I are going to have hard times finding someone to relate to.

Of course, it doesn't make sense to me either. I read my profile, and I want to know him. I read your profile, and would like to know, perhaps, you.

"The most influential book for me has to be *Amusing Ourselves to Death*, by Neil Postman." — I'll take your word, and have to read it.

The most influential book for me was Pär Lagerkvist's *The Eternal Smile*, which I read after locking myself in my room one weekend in high school.

Take my word; you have to read it.

Egbert

Suzie ("nonpareil")

After letting me know through email that she had high standards, and telling me, as a result of my off-the-cuff commentary on Yasujiro Ozu's films, which we were both fans of, that I was brilliant, Suzie picked a midtown restaurant where we arranged to meet each other in person after several weeks of correspondence and telephone conversations. When I declined her offer to share the expense of the meal with her, telling her it was an honor to take her out, she instructed me to figure out where we would go next, that that was up to me.

I was surprised that she did not get it when I said that my car was my chariot. After all, she was a Harvard PhD who had aimed for America from China where previously as a young student she had received the number one score in her province, population one million, on her college entrance exam, I later gathered. Yes, she had high standards.

I thought in my somewhat devious but romantic way to drive Suzie uptown to the Hungarian Cafe where, over twenty years prior, I was in the midst of seducing my then high school-aged companion, now my wife whom I was currently divorcing after two terrible years of marriage, both of whom were Chinese. It was closed, and Suzie asked me offhandedly around midnight in my car if I would like to see Mamaroneck. For all of the ride out of Manhattan into Westchester, I was surprised and not exactly sure what it all meant, even as she chatted in Mandarin with her brother-in-law for directions.

Out of nowhere really, Suzie, who struck me as both high-powered and girlish, as both focused and daring, as both disciplined and sexy, was putting the moves on me. It felt great. This casually stylish, trim, and petite Asian career-woman, a 39-year-old mother of two, had just had a fine and quite expensive meal with a guy and was now inviting him back to her home in the distant suburbs; she was having an unknown man drive her to her house instead of taking the commuter train back home alone. That man, I smiled to myself, was me.

When we got to Mamaroneck, we walked around the neighborhood. I felt enchanted. When we stopped in the street, I felt the happiest I had been in years, and told her so. We kissed outside under the light of a streetlamp. She told me to kiss her the way I drove. She had seen me drive hard and almost crash. She hadn't flinched, nor had I. It was romantic out there, and I felt special to be taken in by this woman whose spirit and desire had taken me unexpectedly.

Because Suzie had small children, I had to leave before they and their nanny woke in the morning. Except for her belly, which I suppose was the result of two childbirths, Suzie was fit and lithe, and she loved being fucked. It seemed as though it had been years since she had been, and I bet it was. I say this only because she was so happy and horny and I really wasn't that good at all.

Everything happened so fast, without notice or preparation; I felt like I was on an inexorable course I had no control over and while the whole thing perplexed me, I couldn't refuse it either.

Everything had been strange. Things often are or turn out to be so with me, so much so that narrating them will again make me believe them. Earlier, for instance, when after dinner Suzie and I were walking west on 54th Street, crosstown to where I had parked my car in a lot, I passed, standing by herself looking into the glass front of a building on an empty sidewalk, Mandy, little blond Mandy, who'd totally freaked out on me, whom I had just slept with a week before. She missed me somehow, and Suzie's hand which was in mine ever since she had taken it, though once she did I told her to take her glove off, I held firmly while I looked bolt ahead.

Being again with a woman who expected as a matter of course me to have sex with her, as had Mandy, while I understood this all to be the successful end to a man's dating fantasy, it threw me off. The suddenly having to deal with being so desired by a woman was almost too much to again take in for me.

I hadn't had to really lift a finger. I hadn't had to act or be anything. I hadn't had to work for anything. I had just been me. A nice me, yes, but just me. And out of the millions and millions of people in New York, I had just been this "me" with two of them far too close in place and time.

After Suzie and I had had sex, she told me that she had decided to bring me back to her house when we were having dinner at the restaurant because of the look in my eyes. True, at that point, I had already myself been taken by her. Her combination of formality and playfulness, her being really smart and at turns delightful turned me on. And I liked the combination, too, of her forcefulness, a directness that came right alongside her gentle Asian beauty. I just plain liked her.

We had clicked. When we were driving back to her house, Suzie had let me know, for instance, that when she went to the restroom at the restaurant, a woman at the table next to us, having seen that I had shaken Suzie's hand when we first greeted each other, inquired during a moment of feminine confidence, if Suzie were on a blind date. "No," Suzie related her having told the woman, "that's just our way. He's always been strange like that."

She also added, to me, that she is not usually so quick on her toes like that. I was charmed by the whole thing. And Suzie, well, her joyfulness over sharing this small, private episode with me made me feel absolutely happy and special.

Thus, it can be through a single moment, a passing tale in the powder room told, that the bonds of intimacy and concupiscence are born.

One of the misfortunes of Suzie's life was that her husband, from whom she had been separated for over three years, had abandoned her and their two very small children to remain an investment banker in Singapore. He, too, was Harvard, but ABD. By chance, the weekend after she and I met, he was back in the States briefly, and wanted to see his children during which time Suzie, after telephoning me, got into her BMW and drove upstate.

She and I had sex three or so times during the afternoon before she drove back to Westchester to scoop up her children. That, at any rate, was the plan. Instead, she called her nanny to receive the children and spent the night with me.

As flattering as this all was to me, hairline cracks were formed. How strange it must have been to the children not to see their mother back? Wouldn't they have questions? Wouldn't they be worried? Wasn't it cold of Suzie? Wasn't it uncaring? Wasn't she basically deserting them? As nice as it was, I began to see that I could not be the man for her.

Still, the following weekend was spent at her home. It was a lovely house. The children were, for a five and two year old, brilliant and articulate. Suzie's home was the living picture of taste and vision. "You can see," she said, "I like expensive things." I acknowledged that I saw that.

Many people with means splash it around, and the result is terrible. Suzie, who came from a country village in China, who spoke flawless English with only the tiniest taste of an accent, knew how to pick objects of value. She knew how to create high-end domestic harmony.

The only thing missing was a husband. The only thing missing was a man. The house yearned for it, creaked for it; it yawned open for it. I felt a place in it opening up for me.

Dinner was hell. The immature antics and nonstop sibling rivalry of two children, the elder, a deserted and hostile boy whose rightful questions spared me only the rod, who openly blamed and condemned his mother for his father being gone, pushed this woman right up to the brink. She did her best, but the disciplinarian had to come out. The usual host of well-meant admonitions and threats that are never followed through on were categorically unleashed; each subsequent transgression of the boy met with an increasingly severe tactical nothing. I sat there totally stifled, paralyzed while German opera continued to pipe through the house.

When the bedroom door opened the following morning while I was on top of the five year old boy's mother, I had to be out of there forever. I pulled the sheet over us quickly so that he could not see that my dick was in her, that we were both naked. I was the man in the vise. I was the spoiler.

And yet, too, I was the man whom this boy had on his own come over to the evening before. And while I lay on the couch resting, I'd been given a kiss, unsolicited, on the cheek. He yearned so badly for a father, it made the timbers of this house creak to the point of almost bursting apart. This whole beautiful house's bones were about to break.

When I got back home, I wrote Suzie a letter letting her know that I could not continue our relationship. I saw very plainly that her children, from whom she had no respite, short of ditching them, were going to very quickly love me. They were already, overnight, forming attachments. There was no way I was going to allow myself to become any further involved in their lives — short of pulling up my own tent stakes and marrying Suzie, which I was not going to do.

I would not allow myself to be the cause of any hurt or harm to these children. I wrote her a kind and caring letter saying goodbye, by hand, and posted it Tuesday.

Out of nowhere, Friday evening, I heard a car pull into my driveway and saw a blue BMW. Suzie was at my front door. Instinctively, I let her in. Keeping my distance, seated in a chair away from her, I told her how angry I was to see her at my house. She was nonplussed. She thought, she said, I'd be happy to see her.

When she started blaming me for leaving her, not giving her an explanation; then faulting me, too, for my letting her into my house if I didn't want her there, when she started to quote kindly meant words I'd written in previous emails against me, I told her I was a hair's breadth away from calling the police.

I could hear how she was thatching things up together. This, I know, is the way the grimmer aspect of how high intelligence works when it feels wronged or injured or wounded. Intelligence can be the poorest servant of delivering one's hurt feelings, and, because in some, like Suzie as in me, because it is so handy and well-trained, the first thing used as the most likely and immediate substitute for expressing them. It builds instantaneously a well-reasoned and logical case that is, of course, totally insane — precisely because it's about thinking, not feeling.

And what can come next is violence when the intelligent consistency of a highly articulate and intelligent person's argument does not persuade or convince the person toward whom it is directed to respond or behave differently, when it does not have its desired effect. Intelligence is supposed to make things happen, and when it doesn't, everything is unpredictable.

Suzie promised me she would not come back again and that this would be it, so, what the hell, with the immediate sense of my being threatened having passed, it was already late, and I liked the idea of sleeping with her one last time. She was here, right? Maybe, too, I liked being desired by someone so much. Maybe I was scared to kick her out. Maybe I just got a little passive. Before she left in the morning, though, I was conscious of one thing: I couldn't get her to agree to much. So, I made her promise me only one thing, that she would never fly again like a bat out of hell to my house if she felt like it, and if she ever had that feeling, she would call me first. She promised this.

One would think that this is where the tale ends. I am sad, and even though I know the outcome, still terrified to write down that even so, it was not over. Nay, the following weekend, after I had received an email now acknowledging from Suzie that everything was all over between us, at about 10:30 at night on Friday, I heard a fist banging my door. Through the glass, I saw it was her.

"Egbert," she said, "can I come in?" I told her "No," and kept the door locked, a custom I am not used to, but had begun of late. I kept it bolted and told her repeatedly as she begged repeatedly that she could not come in my house. She asked just to use the bathroom. I told her there were restaurants downtown. She begged. Through the small windowpanes of my front door, I told her to leave my property. I would sooner let a wild jungle cat into my house than Suzie. I saw her face. She saw mine. I was afraid she was going to break the glass.

Before she was gone, backing out of the driveway very slowly in her BMW, after coming back to the door one last time to ask me to back it out for her, which of course I declined, she had held up some bars of chocolate for me that she had brought. They were Icelandic chocolate, bites of which she had treated and introduced me to at her home in Mamaroneck. They came from Whole Foods, and she had gone back to Whole Foods to get some more for me. At this point, it was bait; at some point, her touch had been caring. She left the brown paper sack of them on my woodpile. I never saw her again.

Suzie had a perfume that on her skin was as delicate and sensuous and lovely as any subtle scent I have ever smelled up close to a woman's neck. She had gotten it at a special *parfumerie* in Paris and was almost out. She'd invited me to go away to Paris with her over Spring Break. Being taken to France by Suzie, Christ! There was great romance in it.

But I also knew I could not be the man in her life nor her children's father. I could not go and purchase in France for her, as I do in my heart wish to, a new bottle of Pergui. I could not do this for a woman before whom I felt cherished, desired, respected, and cared for, so many of the things I have always wanted, but had to for her sake and the children's, even against my own desires to be deeply loved, refuse.

CHAPTER FOUR: PEG ("Winterwithlight")

LETTERS:

Dear Motionmuse

Dear Sweetluvver

Hello Pacifier

Dear Happyhappy

Dear Cherrylix

Dear Mallorcamoon

Honey

Dear moppetpoppet

Dear GoldnGal

Dear Gimmi

Dear Icyeye

Dear Jenjenny

Dear Winterwithlight

STORY: Peg ("Winterwithlight")

Dear Motionmuse:

Let's see:

1) God-fearing. Nope.

2) Willing to pay for a cup of coffee. Yup.

3) Funny & lighthearted. Yup.

4) Krispy Kreme. Nope.

5) Donut. Nope.

6) McDonald's once a year. Yup.

7) Lean, fit, & healthy lifestyle. Yup.

8) Fake teeth. Nope.

9) Gold teeth. See above.

10) Artificially whitened teeth. Nope.

Honestly, though, you don't ask for much; what, may I ask, are you offering?

Egbert

Dear Sweetluvver,

Every fish, or should I say shark, in the ocean is already, I am sure, filling up your mailbox. I have no doubt that you will continue to be up to your eyes and ears in proposals, all of them mostly lies and impossible to fill fabrications. Good luck, however. I believe that you are everything you say you are and exactly who you claim to be.

Egbert

Hello Pacifier,

I am poor Juppi. I am born without shoes. Until I come to United States from Suomi, which you call Finland, I am living all my life at Rovaniemi, which is capital of Lapland. Here in U. S. mountains I am lumberjacking which is a very dangerous work to have. I like very much to have pretty friend someday who have boat like you have. Is this your boat or is this somebody's? You probably do not find my working very interesting to be talking about, so I leave that part of my life story out of the picture of me I am describing. Back at home in Rovaniemi, we have a northern light which at midsummernighttime is very beautiful spectacle for you to visit in your jet if ever you have chance to come visiting us then. You need only to talk of Juppi Jupola, and if I am still in U.S.A. cutting trees, you will become very welcome guest at all streetcorners where a very friendly Finnish people are gathering, which we call ourselves to be Suomalainen, especially when pretty foreign born like you passes by. Here, in U. S. mountains, I not have much luck these days being happy with woman anymore like home. Here, everybody wants to be having so much talking about nothing over and over until it is so late into the nighttime hours and everybody else become so drunken, I only want to sleep. Home, we are very equal people. For wintertime, we go fishing in roundshape hole which we cut in a ice, we drink, and we make sex with each other. Here, I only see drinking. I think you will like me much because you say you have a motto which goes, "Live well, laugh often and love much." This must be a pacific cultural expression I have not heard before today. Please write to me back. I am very lonely and strong Finnish man with so much energy for you to love you very much.

Juppi

Dear Happyhappy,

Nice piece of fiction.

Egbert

Dear Cherrylix:

From tractors (with a matching green outfit!) to an odalisque avec toi un peu, how shall I say, décolleté. I like that. Check me out. OK. Did you click through my pictures? All of them? Did you read me up and down? That's ok. All I care about is, did you catch me, did you catch who I am? I hope so, because there is so much dead weight around here, beautiful-looking driftwood, Christ, I'm getting swamped with vast vats of nothingness. But you, you definitely know how to play. I like that. I like play. C'mon give me a reason to put on my blue velvet jacket. C'mon, let's play.

Egbert

Dear Mallorcamoon,

There is so much longing and desire and yearning on this site, I can barely look at it anymore. You exemplify that longing and desire and yearning. I believe that you are every word that you say. You sound like an incredibly sincere and open person. A man would be lucky to be loved by you. Alas, I can also feel, not only because you live 1000 miles away, that a man like me would simply be too much for you. I will pray for you from time to time, even though I am not in any way religious, that the arms that will eventually hold you will be the arms that love you as you deserve to be loved.

Egbert

Honey,

May I call you that? You've got one of the wackiest profiles I've seen. I hope you never ever give out your phone number, unless it's a cell, to any man you bump into on this site. You've basically said: the taste of Japan repulses me, and everyone (every guy) who's "American," I'm into knowing. The Black Widow catch, the Praying Mantis claws, however, is your education and profession. At least you're honest enough to admit that you came to New York to study the average white criminal mind. Clearly, you like trouble and deviant behavior. But, I confess, I don't want to be *The Fourth Man*, an excellent movie by Paul Verhoeven, but a terrible lifestyle choice. Good luck meeting MEN!

Egbert

Dear moppetpoppet:

You know, I thought the last section of your profile was the lyrics to a Sheryl Crow song, "Now I'm finally free," etc. I'm afraid I've seen your story a thousand million times in the streets of New York: beautiful Asian women with guys who have little lasting desire for them except the fact that they are beautiful Asian women who are willing, no matter what practically, to stay for years and years with these bozos who have little lasting desire for them. Neither person, therefore, can get away from the other. Of course, every couple's story is more complicated than that, but it seems to me that these are the fundamental bricks that so many of these crooked houses are built from, again and again. It's heartbreaking, actually; you, for instance, speak here of essentially being gagged, not talking, kept, because of your perceived language barrier, from speaking; when in fact, you are a talker, a lively (and homesick) thinker. For Christ's sake, you're a talented artist! But, even in your headline, you still refer to yourself as a "poppet," a doll, a plaything. And so long as you continue to retain and project this child's image of yourself, you really cannot be treated as a whole, unified person in your own right, essentially because you yourself have not accepted fully that you are a grown woman, and cannot, therefore, accept virtually anyone who will treat you as such. I'm sorry if that sounds hard, but squirrels trying to cross the road have better luck than people often do getting to the other side of their lives. And there are lots of flattened squirrels in the middle of the road. I'm not really sure what you mean by "someone who's looking for dates for fun." Nobody's looking for someone to push a plow for him. Fun is essential; it is what makes a long term relationship worth keeping. It's what makes the books for children you illustrate worth drawing.

Egbert

Dear GoldnGal,

When I was a boy, I read a folktale about a rock that was in the middle of the road. It sat there unmoved, day after day, for a long time. No one wanted to move it. No one did. It just sat there, an obstruction to travelers passing by who must have, however, maneuvered around this unseemly obstacle. One day, a young man, seeing this impediment to travel, decided to move the stone. Beneath the rock, buried in the ground, was a pot of gold. Seeing only your silhouette in your profile, I wonder if there is something akin to you yourself and this little fable I have related here.

PepperNSaltBoy

Dear Gimmi:

Uh, like, not that I'm into money much myself, but isn't there a huge lake in between what you make and what you want your guy to have? I'm like, granted, you are totally hot, but I want to know just a bit more about you before we go sailing around the word on my seventy-eight foot long yacht.

Egbert

Dear Icyeye:

You speak German? I'm impressed. At first, everyone feels uncomfortable here, I suppose. But after a hundred stabs in the dark that go nowhere except into thin air, a guy gets used to it, and doesn't mind. It's like camping and mosquitoes. You wish there weren't bugs, but there are. It's just part of camping. So, you go with it and pitch the tent, or don't go camping. Welcome to the happy hunting grounds! One small suggestion. See that hunky guy you've not cropped out of that beautiful picture of you? It's not that I'm intimidated or jealous, I'm not, but the sideline of his strong jaw should, in my opinion, be given the big heave-ho. Imagine if I had a picture of me with some sexy bit of two-piece hanging off my sleeve, you know, just enough so that you could see she was really hot. I know, I know, you picked that picture because you look GREAT in it. But you are naturally beautiful, and I'm sure there are dozens and dozens of great pictures of you that will turn any guy's head for the first time. And then there's the never-fail auto-timer function on your camera. Set it, scurry back to your chair, and hold that great look for ten seconds. Transfer to computer. Upload to site. Done.

Egbert

Dear Jenjenny:

I'm sorry, but who is "u"? I'm sorry but you don't give any information, or reveal a single thing about yourself. I don't have any doubt that I am "real." But, I'm sorry, you have not given anything here about you that is even a glimpse of anything "real" at all. All I know from your profile is that you are a 42-year-old, slender, non-white, left-leaning woman who is able to look at my pictures and comments, but I can't see any of yours. Is it any wonder, then, that only jokers and hustlers are contacting you? You might be a really terrific person, but even Prince Charming himself would have to fumble through a haystack for hours and hours and hours to even try to find you. I'm afraid Prince Charming is just going to jump on his horse and ride to the next haystack where maybe a lady with intelligence, beauty, kindness, and warmth will welcome him.

Egbert

Dear Winterwithlight,

I happen to be wearing my favorite gray cashmere hat, my pink and gray hand-knit cashmere scarf, and my gray cashmere sweater right now. I, too, love the feel of it, and have many more scarves of the same (and one small blanket.) All I sleep in are white cotton sheets, and my floors, which I just refinished, are all beautiful and shiny wood that are pleasing to the eye and feel, of course, wonderful underfoot. So, on the purely sensual, it seems as though we hold many of the same cards. It so happens, too, that until I recently erased it, I had a Vermeer for my homepage. Now, it's the late, great Harry Smith.

You mention Sienna; I have been told many times that it is the most beautiful city in Europe. I traveled many, lived in some, but I haven't made it there yet, though someday I will. That, and Dubrovnik...

My life is devoted to writing. In time, if we end up having a conversation, I'd be happy to show you my work which often figures painters (and their paintings themselves) in my texts, from Wyeth to the great canvasses of Kiefer.

As for your opening line in your profile, about beauty and the beholder's eye, I'm a little dazzled, actually, and have woken up the Wordsworth long tucked away: "Behold her, single in the field, Yon solitary Highland Lass." You have stopped me cold in my tracks.

Egbert

Peg ("Winterwithlight")

I had Japanese food with Peg and, even though she had offered at the end of our lackluster date to pay for half, I countered by paying for the whole. After all, it was thirty bucks and I didn't feel like figuring out how much to tip and all that with her. It just wasn't worth the fifteen or sixteen or seventeen bucks it was going to cost me not to have done that.

After all, I had blown it right from the start when this lithe and green-eyed Scottish beauty had said, almost as the first thing when we sat down, that I looked much younger than my pictures, and much better than them too. No, I couldn't say: "Thank you. And while you are no doubt a great beauty, you look your age of 46, the same age as me," or something along those lines, which was basically the only thing I could think of at the moment. That pause after her compliment, my male lack of a response where one was due, where it was pretty much obligatory, just to be courteous actually, was pretty much all telling.

I have to say, too, that her speaking in all sorts of esoteric-philosophical ways about her work as a painter; and my expressing my reluctance to show her any of my work as a writer — over my own set of esoteric-philosophical reasons, all of which were just as true and truth-seeking as were hers in explaining to me her *ars poetica* — didn't help. We were two artists, and we did not match at all.

I probably blew it before that even when I was five minutes late meeting her in Union Square due to my having been stuck standing in the express line across the street at Whole Foods to buy twenty bucks of chocolate. Nothing, before meeting a woman you are interested in, should ever hold you up or be a priority over her; and telling Peg that that's what I had done, which, if one has done such a thing in the first place, one in the second place then never confesses to, I also did.

It made me seem lackadaisical, which, in retrospect, I suppose I was. We just went through politely the motions of a date. It all must have gone through her like an arrow, one that did not pierce her; it just went in and went out. No bleeding, no pain, much of little felt.

Afterwards, we sent each other cordial emails that confirmed that there was nothing there.

CHAPTER FIVE: AMÉE ("Diamondmind")

LETTERS:

Karen, whoah

Dear Stacey

Hi, Goldenwoman

Dear Smileagain

Dear Freedom101

Hi, Silkworm

Hi, JetSetter

Hi, Snakecharmer

Dear Spink

Hi, Lovelylulu

Dear Diamondmind

STORY: Amée ("Diamondmind")

Karen, whoah!

How did you get away with that panty shot! I couldn't even get these Matchheads to post the TOTALLY innocent head-shot I wanted as my primary photo because there must have been too much diffuse white light in the background or something. You definitely must have dated somebody on the inside. I've looked at a few hundred of these two-fisted sob stories, and NO ONE has used "FULL PACKAGE" except you. What's your secret? Let me know.

Egbert

Dear Stacey,

You described me to a tee. But skipped right by. How come?
It's ok. Seriously. I stopped expecting anything from this site.
Please, I beseech you, don't take that with any negative scent.
There isn't any. It just appears to me that the moment anything more than the usual humdrum, "I'm a well-rounded,
laid-back gentleman looking for an attractive woman looking to definitely have two children" appears up on the screen,
the horseman zips by that lamppost. You said you wanted a
"a dragon-slayer, a shape-shifter, a warrior"; well, my actual
name, not my pseudo Finno-Ugric one, means, in one particular context, "shape-shifter." But, all that is just too upfront
and overboard and vibrant, to use a pretty dead word, to
describe myself here. I do have to say, though, I don't get the
wink thing. I'd never wink at Uma Thurman in a bar, and I
wouldn't wink at you. I mean, it's like you've been maunder-
ing in my ear already with your very to the point profile; and
my feeling is if a guy doesn't know what he wants to say to
you by this point, it's pretty hopeless. Please, I also hope that
you understand that I'm really not looking to meet anyone
anymore. I look at this place where maybe a nice quick conversation can happen at the depot before either your or my
bus comes. And then, one of us gets on.

Egbert

Hi, Goldenwoman:

There are two things I don't quite understand in your profile. You say, on the one hand that you are "ordinary," yet you have a PhD. You say, too, that "we all like to date beautiful people with little else," but you are definitely looking, it seems, for someone who has a lot of other positive qualities than merely being attractive. While you are certainly a beauty yourself, it's obvious from your poise and interests and education that you seek someone who is compatible in both intellect and in his sense of compassion. Seeing the bright golden locket hanging from your neck in both pictures, which appears from its luster to be a Buddhist figure that you wear all the time, and the flowers that appear behind you in the background — these details, along with your words, make it plain that you are a sincere and balanced woman who is centered both spiritually and physically. I hope you consider taking a second look at my profile and drop me a note, for, like you, I strive to do things for myself that are good for both my mental and physical health, too, and identify with the more profound sense of beauty I think you seek and try in your life to create.

Egbert

Dear Smileagain,

I'm afraid I'm not simple the way you wanted in your profile. But, I'm a lot of the other things. To tell you the truth, though, I am not really looking to meet anyone here. I do remember that great movie with Angie Dickinson, too, from the 70's, I think it was. It was a stunner. I saw that you're a CIA grad. I once knew a girl in college; she was actually a friend of a girl in college, who instead of going to college went to cooking school, and I remember being impressed about how she knew exactly what she wanted to do with her life at a very young age, unlike me who has lived a basically peripatetic life for a great deal of it. I hope, because I have tried, at any rate, to communicate with you 150%, just as you had hoped for in a man. It'd be nice to chat here a little bit, but really ok, if not, as well, since I don't have any real expectations. Good luck!

Egbert

Dear Freedom101,

I've pretty much thrown the towel in here. When I say weird stuff like, "My dad used to needlepoint Mondrian pictures," people don't write me back. And when I say general, nice stuff they hardly do either. So, I've given up actually meeting anyone. I mean, there are so many pretty and beautiful and well-educated women, I thought it'd be fairly easy to, at least, get a conversation going about Radiohead, but it isn't. It's next to impossible, even that. But, I'm trying, I'm trying!

Egbert

P.S. your clothes color coordination next to that Mondrian you're up against really is very funny.

Hi, Silkworm,

I've basically given up on all of this. I'm writing you now because you sound smart and clear. To tell you the truth, I'm really not all that gung ho and concerned about meeting; if it should eventually happen with you or anyone, then it does. But if all it amounts to is to have exchanged an email or two back and forth, I'm glad enough to have learned a little from you and to have shared a little back.

Egbert

Hi, JetSetter,

I'm too young for you, according to your profile, by a couple of years. To tell you the truth, though, I'm not really thinking of meeting anyone here. Maybe, then, it's only to say that I read your profile and like how obviously determined and picky you are. I think the shots of you by the piano are great, and I'm always impressed by people who take care of themselves as you obviously do. I can't imagine, at most, your dropping me more than a line, especially since I don't even live in NYC at all, and tend to shop on the West Coast when I'm out there anyway.

Egbert

Hi, Snakecharmer,

Your profile has popped up a whole bunch of times, and I haven't written you because I really don't think of myself as laid back. To tell you the truth, I'm not sure what that means. With all those activities going on, like rollerblading (not the way I understand very laid back), I might not understand it at all. But if it means just a night with a Netflix movie, then I've got it. Or some lazy something or other. But, to tell you the truth, I don't even think about actually meeting anyone on Match anymore, I've gotten so laid back about it all. Maybe we'll trade a couple of emails, and wish each other well, is about the best or most that'll happen. And I'm pretty ok with that anyway.

Egbert

Dear Spink,

I've pretty much given up on this whole thing. Everyone I look at is pretty and full of brains and all sorts of generally good qualities. How did all this happen? So, I think pretty much the most I expect is an email or two back and forth, the kind of well-wishes you give cousins boarding a ship for a year long cruise around the world. Any thoughts?

Egbert

Hi, Lovelylulu,

I'm not trying to meet you. I only wanted to say that you look really healthy and happy.

Egbert

Dear Diamondmind:

I never fail at anything.

The first girl I slept with went to Yale.

The first woman I married works at Yale.

The second woman I married. Went to Yale.

But my first wife went to Brown.

And the second woman I'm divorcing.

And the first girl I slept with has found me.

I never fail at anything.

Egbert

Amée ("Diamondmind")

When I finally met Amée, she was out of her mind and I was in my element. I say "finally" because Amée and I had been in touch about this whole Match thing of mine, my crazy project, almost since I had first made contact with her. Almost immediately, she felt like a sister to me, so anything was game: high, low; vulgar & literary; it didn't matter.

Tattooed up and down her arms, pale, thin, and elegant, she was pouring wine into little plastic glasses with her Elvis Costello-y boyfriend-slash-fiancé for her art opening in New Haven. Maddest of all was that this guy quickly related to me that he'd been diagnosed with an alcohol abuse disorder about two weeks prior and here he was pouring the grape. I could see this trainwreck coming and kept the binoculars in my pocket.

Now, Yale and I have a special connection. My first girlfriend, the one I slept with, went there as an undergrad. She'd ditched me at the beginning of September, like a puppy suburbanites leave on the side of the highway after they're done with summer, and went back to her previous thespian Greek scholar boyfriend she'd broken up with. I've never really felt the pain of that to tell you the truth, though I'm still trying. As it turns out, the girl I married in secret and told nobody about, a Brown/Stanford PhD, now works in special collections at Yale.

And, too, my most recently divorced wife got her Master's in Architecture there. In my initial email to Amée, I told her all this, quite succinctly, in a wry little spot of verse, and she commented on my rather poor track record with Yale girls. I countered: Was she kidding me? My record, I said, was perfect.

At her MFA opening, all night long Amée basically kept saying over and over, "I am so fucking tweaked," and basically vulgarizing everybody she came in contact with. When, however, there was this medical school chick I was hitting on, Amée cleaned up her act lickety-splickety just like a girl who can get all the pot smoke out of her bedroom right before Mom is knocking and turning the doorknob, and make it look like she's been studying stuff like mitochondria and ATP for some AP Bio exam she's taking tomorrow. Amée wanted to help me. I loved her. Amée was all class and presentation, as glamorous and naturally so as they come.

Picture me in the art building on Chapel Street with a camera shouting at some girl, another painter, a classmate of Amée's, in front of her gigantic pink picture, shouting at her among tons of people just to get one good shot. I like doing shit like that. Nobody likes being shouted at, and people like even less if in a picture what will be captured is the look of them being shouted at. I know this. The results of these bizarre tactics are stupendous.

And the beauty is that I don't even belong there. Only through the passkey of Amée, wild out of her mind with garbage and thinking and shit that I could go on about for a coupla nights easily nonstop with her, was I legit there. That was all it took. One artist, one guest. All it ever does.

Her boyfriend, well, he confessed that he had some rage issues. Now that Amée had finished her degree, he was going to do his in writing at Columbia. They were going to get married; it seemed to work, and they'd get housing, an issue because, now that Amée's stint in the big leagues was complete, where was there to go except back to Florida or being a barista? Marriage and housing was the answer. Jack, her beau, with whom I also hung, said to me, "I have a very strong voice." And, I wanted to say to this lad, "Can you write your own Will & Testament, too?" Unless he was hiding in his underpants some insane package I couldn't see,

Amée was going eat and destroy this little sonovabitch before Whitsunday, was all I could say to myself.

I was never in any way attracted romantically to Amée. She was beautiful, smart as a whip, a fucking raging artist, independent, fearless, and totally cracked me up. You'd give her twenty bucks if she needed it just because she'd asked for it. She smoked & drank, and I do not. Who cares? I don't know, I think in the end, I was looking for someone actually softer and gentler, someone toward whom I felt being soft and gentle to to be with. Amée was a whole bunch of pieces to my rock-apple pie, and even though I never heard from her again after I drove off at around eleven P.M. dead tired back home to New York, I think the world of her. She was a really cool chick.

CHAPTER SIX: JEAN ("Pinkroadster")

LETTERS:

Dear Holdingyourhand

Hi, Twobirdsinhand

Dear Nono525

Dear Goomal

Hi Pepperjackie

Dear Felicia

Unfortunately, Hangtenwithme

Dear Annieshortbread

Hi, Pinkroadster [1]

Dear Pinkroadster [2]

STORY: Jean ("Pinkroadster")

Dear Holdingyourhand,

That's sweet that the only turn-ons you clicked were "Candlelight" and "Dancing." It paints a very romantic picture of your heart. Alas, I am not very much of a dancer, and my stride is 3000 miles across the country anyway. How did I find you? Just sort of followed a trail of breadcrumbs, I suppose. Too bad you don't live across the street; too many people get the goofy side knocked out of them with a lot of education and brains. And even fewer desire to make the rest of life unimportant if they have found a way to embrace the world with true love. Good luck finding the man who holds you in his arms while the two of you dance on a snow-capped mountaintop.

Egbert

Hi, Twobirdsinhand,

At the risk of sound banal, I found your no foolin' around assertiveness refreshing — especially, I'll say again, in contrast to all the drek I've read. You sound like an actual person with clear tastes and dislikes. Why is that such a big deal to announce? I can't for the life of me understand why anybody giving this site a spin would fail to do so. These are like pre-diplomatic meetings; some cards need to be shown. Otherwise, we're all just pretty butts and brightly colored underpinnings, if I may use your phrases. I am curious, though, what's with the aviary? It's in your pictures and your metaphors you use to explain yourself (nest, bower, bird). It's still really sad that you as a woman have to write that you are looking for a man who doesn't mind that she can fix things. Doesn't mind? Maybe I'm guilty of reverse-sexist pandering: I'd be turned on if you could sweat pipes and sharpen a chainsaw. I ain't just innerested in yer cookin them blueberry pancakes fer me in the mornin, honey. Oh, it's a really nice bit about embracing while sleeping; it paints a sweet picture. I was, however, jolted a little bit about your line over wanting to "grow old with"; I'm not in denial or anything, but the literalness of that, that we all are growing old, getting older, and going, to be, inshallah, some day very, very old, was a wake up. One final thing, I've never said it myself, but you have here. It's a contrast! I definitely am NOT a beach person; I am a woods person. I'd never thought about or realized that I was dealing with a potential duality here: sand or dirt. Thanks for bringing that home to me.

Egbert

Dear Nono525,

Help me out. I can't tell what you mean in your profile by "get me." Do you mean like understand you "get me" or the other kind? Maybe I don't get you, or maybe I do. But I'm on the fence between something that's somewhat intellectual and something that's not. I know I'm way out there, but where are you?

Egbert

Dear Goomal:

I saw *Slumdog Millionaire* last night and it filled me such a feeling of self-disgust, I almost left several times before it was over. But, I stayed and wrapped up my understanding of it under these two words: vanity and voyeurism.

More than anything else, the film made me feel my own incredible vanity. It made me feel the baseness of my always being after the smartest and most beautiful woman, the best computer, the fastest car. It made me feel the absolute foolishness of what really amounts to my own petty and bourgeois desires. Even here (especially here) on Match, for instance: I am determined to make myself appear the smartest and most insightful man to the smartest and most educated woman I can possibly appeal to; you, in this instance, even as I diminish myself with calculated self-loathing; all of which naturally serves to speak, in the end, well of me as a person who is at least capable of some degree of self-awareness — and therefore, truly desirable.

But what does it really mean? I am basking in the luxury of my own pretentiousness, hunting online for a soulmate, a lover, a partner, a lifelong companion, because, on my Macintosh computer, seated in my antique Amish chair, in my cute little renovated house with shiny wood floors and fancy dimmer switches, I have the leisure time to do so — to while away my time, picking and choosing, writing to infinitely attractive women like you, most of whom will not even consider dropping me a note back (for which I do thank you for having done already); and those who do, and with whom I have had the good fortune to date once or twice, they are all richly educated and deeply intelligent like me, before, like the passing of a summer shower, the brevity of our knowing each other passes with little casualty and small eventual effect, not even so modest as a mild case of food poisoning.

In the face of the total and outright squalor depicted in *Slumdog*, I am only embarrassed. There I was, like you, with India's colorful slums as the backdrop, its teeming poor being shown for my moviegoing entertainment and perhaps amusement. Or, even worse, to actually feel, for a brief two hours, the seething hardship of millions of others, to feel in my heart the pain of the sordid wretchedness of these castaway lives, before hopping in my silver stick shift Saab to drive in unimpeachable comfort fast back home, feeling, perhaps, too, that something "real" had happened to me. Truly, to view the actual landscape of India's ruined poor is far more shameful than any bout or overdose of pornography; for the movie mistakenly makes, I think, its audience feel a sort of "moral truth," when, in fact, all that has occurred is a sort of moral prurience. At least pornography does not vaunt itself as being anything more than it is; it never claims, never pretends, and is never expected to be at the service of any purpose higher than itself.

Now, it is also possible that the moviemakers of *Slumdog* knew exactly what they were doing, and, quite conscious of who the viewing audience would largely be — the broad swath of middle class occidentals — they intended in their film to mock the likes of you and me. For, after all, if you put aside all the knee-jerk Judeo-Christian guilt that presupposed the above take on the movie, the movie was suffused with joyful people largely living joyfully; and if not joyfully, at least they were actually living their lives! They were not numbed and they had not succumbed to routine lives (forgive me this) of "work, gym...[and] hanging out"; they were not trying to find some "spark" to "ignite" the torpor of their otherwise, to all appearances, highly accomplished and successful lives — as both you and I are doing, it seems to me. No, it is only when the lives depicted in *Slumdog* began to resemble our own, with the rising pile of material accoutrements, did the characters' lives correspondingly sink down into the morass of being quickly deadened. It seems, then, that it is only when you verily have insurance for your life, like the ripped off American couple with insurance for their stripped car, that it is suddenly bereft of meaning. That is the savage mockery and commentary *Slumdog* may have been making on its viewers in America who "loved" it, but alas, did not, sadly, for all their overweening intelligence and cross-cultural savvy, get. Not in the slightest. Not at all.

I'd love to hear your reply!

Egbert

Hi Pepperjackie,

You sound, on the surface, like a powerhouse of ambition and control. I suppose the latter sounds almost negative, but I don't mean it to be value-laden like that. Rather, you lay your cards down 1, 2, 3, 4. It's quite upfront and certain, I suppose, to ward off the bikini gawkers eyeballing your tummy.

While I am certainly someone with an artistic edge, financially secure, modern, and forward-thinking, etc., I'd be hard put to say I'd go out on a date with anyone whose preconditions are marriage and children. Honestly, it sounds very cart before the horse to me, making dating a sort of promissory note to be cashed in at such-and-such date. Doubtless, though, as you do stand out as quite beautiful and certainly well-educated, many a would-be husbands will seek to run their fingers through your lock of bleached hair, which is testimony, I suppose, to your streak, as it were, of iconoclasm and overall limelighting incandescent self.

Should you choose to write back to me, we may after a few volleys, swap phone numbers — but not on the first serve. Oh, by the way, as you mention in your profile, and as often turns out not to be case, my pictures are all up to date; I am fit, lean, toned, and look like them.

If I do not hear back from you, I'd go a little more softly… with your beauty and brains, a woman like you deserves more than a banker who's just going to reciprocate with financial security and marital hardball.

Egbert

Dear Felicia,

About four days ago, I was in the grocery store and a girl, about six or seven, asked her mother, "How come there are watermelons now?" I was standing to their side in the deli line, and the mother replied, "Some people like them." It was the perfectly wrong answer of course. What the girl was actually asking her mother was: Why are there watermelons, which we eat during the summertime, in the grocery store now during the wintertime? I had to resist the obvious urge to bend down a little and say to the little girl, "Well, the planet is like a big ball. And there are places on it right now where the sun is shining and it's summer. The reason we have watermelons here now, is that they fly them from places on the planet where it's summer right now to where it's winter." I didn't. I didn't know the two. It was one of those everyday social barriers that usually is better kept. Asking strangers in an elevator if they've all filed their taxes at the end of April is not good public etiquette. I did say to the mother, though, as I was handed my half-pound of sliced mesquite turkey, "She asks good questions." "Which questions?" she asked me. "The one about the watermelons," I said. "Yes, she sure does," she said smiling.

A week ago, I was riding up the ski lift. A father with a pretty hardcore macho man accent was talking to his two little boys. It was just after lunch. The boys were about eight and five. "Let's shoot at three," the older boy said. "OK," said the dad, "we'll shoot at three." The two boys and father continued talking about "shooting" at three or two but not four. In my parlance, they meant, let's try to go at about three o'clock, let's try to aim for then; I realized that these weren't little boys: they were little men. The father continued talking about getting back to base, and the space they needed to keep between the quads in the dark. He was talking about the three of them riding ATV's, or All Terrain Vehicles, undoubtedly to some rustic log cabin in the hinterland. I sat quietly, the fourth person in the squished chair, with my bright blue jacket and crash helmet and skis dangling. I realized that all the boys' metaphors were around hunting and killing. Real Hemingway. But, there was something far more important. These two little boys adored their father. They loved him. He was out with them. I wanted to pull the dad aside just after we were spilled out of the chair at the mountaintop, pull him lightly by his collar, like a lover would, and tell him in a whisper, "You know, your boys really love you."

These are a couple of anecdotes that I've tapped out just now in reply to your profile about liking to hear stories. You look and sound like a very warm and lovely person; I hope you write me back.

Egbert

Unfortunately, Hangtenwithme,

I have a cat; otherwise, I'd write you a letter as long as it took Homer to send Odysseus back to Ithaca. I would sing to you of seas, and adventures, and longings. But that is not meant to be.

All I can say, then, ever so prosaically, is that you sound and look like a totally wonderful person; and I am sure you are everything and more than you state you are.

Bon voyage!

Egbert

Dear Annieshortbread:

Thanks for the consideration, but I don't feel as though we'd make a good match.

Good luck!

Egbert

Hi, Pinkroadster,

I used to play this game that you might like to try yourself. I did it with the GRE. Blot out the question itself, and choose the right answer from the five answers alone. You'll be surprised! Get back to me, after digging out your LSAT and GMAT stuff or what have you. I mean, if you're all alone and it's 2 A.M., there are definitely worse things a boy could do with himself, or a girl, for that matter. In any case, it sure beats the boredom and superficiality of life I can see you're actively avoiding, in your camo outfit, knees wide, and drinking or drunk in half your pictures. Honestly, please don't get me wrong, I think you're funny as hell, and if you're just over half as conceited and stuck up as I am, I think we might have a good future, or a handful of weekends, if things don't work out, making French toast, stir fry this and that, and salmon with cayenne on it together — or whatever you've got in mind. And at night, we can cuddle up with some Princeton Review special *chez vous* or mine upstate.

Egbert

Dear Pinkroadster:

Please complete the following Match Guy Aptitude Test (MGAT). When finished, please submit your answers to me for correction.

Thank you.

Egbert

1.   The guy on Match is
        a)   nice but insincere
        b)   bright but not brilliant
        c)   dull but not dumb
        d)   forward-thinking but not revolutionary
        e)   eager but not crazy

2.   The guy on Match lives
        a)   too far away to commit
        b)   too far away to love
        c)   too close for me to see other guys
        d)   far away enough to miss me when he's not here
        e)   around the block

3.   The guy on Match is probably
        a)   a faithful and romantic man at heart
        b)   a two-bit sonovabitch at heart
        c)   a tranny
        d)   a trust fund alcoholic
        e)   a dangerous sociopath

4.   I like the guy on Match because
     a)   he will eat of my hand, night or day
     b)   he's cute enough for now
     c)   he's original and daring, even at his own expense
     d)   he's rich and famous
     e)   someone I know dated him already

5.   Most guys on Match
     a)   suck
     b)   have great six-packs
     c)   are virgins
     d)   are cultured, worldly, and speak several languages
     e)   know how to make a girl laugh

6.   The guy on Match probably likes me because
     a)   like me, he's thinking about law school
     b)   like me, he's thinking about medical school
     c)   like me, he's thinking about becoming a chartered financial analyst
     d)   I wrote him back already one time
     e)   he just thinks I'm beautiful, funny, and smart

7.   Going out on a date with the guy on Match would probably lead to
     a)   the feeling that I was being listened to by someone who cares about what I have to say
     b)   both of us seeing what the other is like
     c)   my talking to him about stuff that makes me happy as well as concerned
     d)   unexpected sex with him all night long until the pigeons are cooing
     e)   a belief in love, even if it doesn't seem practical

8. Even if in the end it doesn't work out for me and the guy on Match, I will be happy to have known him because
    a) he will have been kind and gentle to me
    b) he will have been a solid lover with a great body
    c) he will have made me feel good about myself
    d) he will have made me realize or affirm that not all guys are shitheads
    e) all of the above

9. My number one reservation about going out on a date with the guy on Match is
    a) I actually think guys are pretty yucky
    b) he's way older than I am
    c) I don't think he can really be serious about me
    d) I'm actually afraid of finding a really good guy
    e) I'd like to keep this Match-thing at a distance

10. If I were to go out on a date next weekend with the guy from Match, I'd tell him I'd be comfortable going to
    a) that falafel place on Avenue A
    b) the Pegu Club in Soho
    c) Katz's on Houston for pastrami sandwiches
    d) anyplace uptown for coffee
    e) to dinner somewhere in the Meatpacking District

Jean ("Pinkroadster")

The first thing Jean was concerned with when I met her for coffee in White Plains was how she appeared to me; that is, did I mind that she was much plainer in person than she had been in the picture she had put up of herself online. That is, until she had changed her photo for another the night before. That is, did I mind that she had done that? That is, could I like her this way?

Before that, she was absolutely, drop dead stunning. In person, she was attractive enough, but no head-turner. I wouldn't have thrown her out of bed, nor would I have taken her home to Mom and Dad. Still, it's embarrassing when no sooner than two people from Match do meet, they start analyzing Match itself. It means it's dead in the water: if that, Match itself is the only thing two people can muster up to talk about together, if the only common denominator between two people is the online dating service they used to bring them together, and to discuss their past experiences, all of which *ipso facto* must not have worked out, then there is equally as little promise they will either.

Still, I remained intellectually curious to hear Jean, a well-paid accountant, break down in percentages the men she found eligible candidates. Just by showing up, by my not cancelling at the last minute, or wishing to change the date, I realized, by her reckoning, I was already in the top 10%.

From there, though, the odds seemed to decrease exponentially. There, in that last 2 1/2%, by keeping to schedule and my word, is where Jean let me know I happened to be. Somewhere there she was being saved, by her own calculations, it seemed, for some lucky sonovabitch who'd give her the whole farm and a promissory note for collateral.

She told me a tale of being taken out to an expensive steak dinner by a Wall Street executive. When he asked her, she related, "Do you like sex?" she stopped at appetizers, claiming to the gentleman that she was no longer hungry. Her point, I suppose, was to show me she had morals, and that she would not take a man for one single steak if she found his values repellent or unattractive.

"What," she asked me, "do you think about a question like that?" Naturally, hoping not to just as abruptly end our date at the cafeteria-style coffeehouse we were seated at, not at some fancy joint where the big boys pumped up their cholesterol and balls over a thick slab of Angus, I concurred with Jean's assessment; without, at the same time, wholly condemning my own semi-salacious and libidinous tendency, so as not to possibly, however slim the chance, find myself in a contradictory bind of logic I could not surmount should the evening pan out in such a way that I was questioned again by Jean over wherefore my fingertips were prowling at the top of her underpants.

But this, I doubted, would ever happen: for by her bringing up the past steakhouse episode and the serious affront to her character it had caused her then, now being displayed as a lesson to me through symbolic narration meant clearly that her response, had she responded to the gentleman in question over her liking of sex, would have have to have been "No"; and if not "No" itself, then something punitive for sex with her, something like offering to her the stars and moon and one's firstborn's toenail clippings drowned in Aramaic vinegar and then sealed forever in amber in order to get her pants off, would be required.

She took me entirely wrong when I suggested we go somewhere else to continue our talk. She felt interrupted, dislodged, and altogether, I suppose, minimized. My forehead was hot from all the intellectual fervor. I just needed a change of location, I tried to explain to her, along with an unnecessary apology, as she now stood on the curb of the sidewalk and pointed to the direction she was crossing to, and pointed to the direction perpendicular from hers, where she told me I was to go.

CHAPTER SEVEN: CINDY ("Oceanlife")

LETTERS:

Hi, Atlantagirl

Hi, Cityzipper

Dear Celia05

Hi, Zn727

Hi, Readingglasseson

Dear Angie2008

Hi, Snowsonnet

Dear Scarlettdewdrop

Hi, Bespoken13

Dear Petitelune

Dear Caroline8

Hi, Oceanlife

STORY: Cindy ("Oceanlife")

Hi, Atlantagirl,

I must confess, it is hard to imagine how anybody could lie to you, as you write about in your profile. You look like the sort of person who would just melt a lie right out of a man's mind. Even though you do not reveal a great deal in your profile, you sound so sweet and genuine; I come back to the same question for you as I have for myself: what on earth ever happened in my life that I ended up here? You see, it's pretty obvious, in just this little glance into you, that you're a special person — and so am I. How do people like us end up searching for someone who gets us? How did we ever end up with people in our lives who did not? I'm not saying that you and I will ever end up together, but we're both attractive, good people. There are many like us. Maybe, as you say, after we talk some day, I'll be able to describe you to yourself as more than just a beautiful, sunshine-filled woman with a heart as sweet as her mango colored dress. Maybe someday, you'll be able, also, to describe me to me.

Best,

Egbert

Hi, Cityzipper:

Actually, what you have to write is everything and the only thing I have to go by. The thought of sending pictures of my body is so absurd to me. I'm embarrassed that you have to write not to do it. Apparently, there are enough (or so many) dolts in the world that you must have found it necessary to do so.

What especially caught my attention in your profile was how you were better educated by your parents than by teachers and professors. It's smart. It reveals that you value depth and wisdom, without diminishing the importance of education. There's something very clear in your writing about the importance of being a consistent and attentive person, not just some cocky joker who believes a dozen roses will win your heart. They're nice, but the intention of the hand holding them out to you is what matters, and is what ultimately counts in the world. One man can give you a hundred dozen roses, and every petal means little or nothing; another could give you a single bloom, and from him, it will mean the world.

I hope to hear back from you. You sound like a serious, sincere, intelligent person who definitely wants and expects the same. I hope you're playful, too, because I'm certainly that as well!

Best,

Egbert

Dear Celia05:

You wrote, "Someone who thinks it's romantic to work on his own thing in the same room as me."

That's the catch. That's the thing. The idea of being able to do my work, and you yours in the same room is terribly romantic. It means you get each other. You feed off the quiet presence of each other. You do not interrupt, nor need to constantly tap the other on the shoulder for validation. Just their presence does that. To be able to be that, do that, is the full moon of real romance. Who else could you possibly do this with besides someone you totally trust? No one.

As for Cormac McCarthy, let's save that one for later. But for starters, my answer is: It's a two-part question beginning with your presupposition that he is a great American writer. As for American Democracy, well, that decline began with the direct election of Senators rather than their election by the House. The decline in Democracy is probably inversely proportional to the rise of advertising or mass-publicity. But these are just some conversations I'd love to have with you.

Trust me, I'm way unconventional, highly opinionated and fiercely analytical (thus, I can back up what I say). For instance, *Slumdog Millionaire*? I will declaim that movie with maximum condemnation until, even if you know how to cross the Pacific without vomiting, you'll be sick of hearing my argument! (I will, however, certainly listen to yours, intelligently).

Oh, I am ginger ADDICT. Ginger snaps. Ginger beer. Ginger tea (only from the root.) Please, yes, cook them for me! And Earl Grey, yes, with a sprig of mint! Lovely.

Long live the PLANET Pluto!

Egbert

Hi, Zn727:

Where you have ended up living, I ended up leaving: I grew up in Greenwich. If we should meet, I can take you on a "quiet walk" down the road where my house is. There's a beach at the end of it, past the white gates on Byram Shore Road. It looks out over the Sound and is lovely.

I'm afraid I wouldn't be able to suggest where to have an "intimate dinner," however. Much has changed since I moved away. I'd have to leave that up to you. I'm sure you could pick a wonderful place.

Egbert

Hi, Readingglasseson:

You don't come off "scary" at all. You're smart and alive. I am intense and don't even realize I'm not letting up. To me, it's just passion. But, lest I come across as some headball, I am, at the same time, as playful as a jester taking down the king. I always mean business, never get my head cut off, and usually have a twinkle in my eye. I will never ever be your nightmare. Not the re-hashing the day, honey, way. Never. Not like that. I'd choke myself to death before anything like that happened. I do hope you write me back.

Egbert

Dear Angie2008:

It is bad manners, I hate to tell you, to do work, such as checking your messages, when someone else is giving his personal time to be with you at dinner. You shouldn't, though, as you say, apologize: it should never happen. Period. Ever. It's just good grooming. It's just good breeding. It's just being well brought up. Wherever you were brought up, I am sure people know that. It means simply that you value someone else's time over your work. It means that you have balance in your life. It means that you can create boundaries, first of all for yourself. Time for work. Time for love. Time for everything. A Psalms and a Peter, Paul & Mary kind of thing. Both the religious side and the hippy-dippy people agree on this one.

Of course, you are right about the gym and guys making a big deal of it; still, I'm afraid that of the over five hundred women's profiles I have read thus far, yours is the only one to start off talking about the gym and then go off on it for half a paragraph. Strange fruit, indeed. But, honestly, what in God's good name can you expect when the second word out of your mouth here is "useless"? "Embarrassed," you claim. Ashamed. Pained. Hurt.

You make my heart ache: you are so beautiful and obviously intelligent, and yet you sound so cold and mean-spirited. I don't think you get it, but your supposedly concealed innermost feelings that you proclaim you don't want to wax on about, are spilled all over the place like fish guts here. Is that all you really want, to waste time, to leave some guy who's opened up to you, who might be half in love with you (it does happen, you know), just to cross him off, like an enemy, killed like time under your breath while you brush your teeth and shake out the bristles for the night? You are totally right about one thing: guys in jeans and white sneakers. Yuck, it's the uniform of pedophiles in Thailand kind of thing. Except for the latter sneaker stuff, your profile is one knot after the next of contradiction, from the bottom to the top.

Egbert

Hi, Snowsonnet,

You already have an amazing life and sound like an amazing woman. You're fit, healthy, beautiful; you sail, ski, hike, ride. Me, I'd be right alongside you. You're the only person I've run across on this site who genuinely sounds and looks like she's in better shape than I am. And I don't mean that to sound boastful; rather, it's a compliment to you. And, on top of that, I love the picture of you at the piano. I play, too, by the way — just some of Beethoven's easy sonatas, Bach, and easier Mozart and the like, if you know what I mean. But it makes me happy, of course. On top of all that, you read (or, as you say, "listen") to the classic books. And your music choice is far-ranging.

Can any man keep up with all the things you do? You sound so incredibly alive and invigorating, I couldn't resist. If you think you'd like to jack my iPod, as I could definitely listen to the music on yours, drop me a line, as you suggested I have you.

Egbert

Dear Scarlettdewdrop:

I can't imagine what kind of dope would not want to get in some "fun" time with you. You are about nineteen different things in one person. Just as you say, you sound feisty and full of fire. And, not to get all creepy on you, you are easily both the sexiest and most beautiful woman I've stumbled across on this site. I love that you're a camping and fishing girl — it makes you real. A beautiful Italian-Irish tomboy who looks Korean but isn't. Totally amazing.

You sound like a real person, and you look like a goddess. Are these guys you mention in passing out of their minds!!!? Me, well, for your proclaimed taste, I'm way older than you're looking for. But that doesn't bother me a bit, and it certainly won't stop me. I definitely take care of myself; I'm superfit, but no muscle-building freak. I am fashionably neat, and like how handsome I am. Which is not the same thing as vanity. And, as you like it, I drive REALLY fast. I love driving fast, and leaving other people in the dust.

I hope to hear back from you. Any guy with a mind and sense would realize, if he were ever with you, that you're the only fun he ever, ever needed for his whole life.

Egbert

Hi, Bespoken13,

I can't believe I'm going to say this (since I'm going to basically shoot myself in my own foot), but you appear pretty and bored enough to go out with some joker who's not at all serious about anything except that you're very pretty and sound bored enough to try anything. Now, I'm no joker, and obviously hope you'll believe that and write me back; but, I'd prefer that you'd be overcautious and pass over me as good practice for the jerk-offs out there who are.

Your Guardian Angel with a Conflict-of-Interest,

Egbert

Dear Petitelune,

Unfortunately, my little moon, all the oafs and con artists have given the gallantry of true gentlemen bad names. Were I to present myself a perfect scoundrel, I'd have better luck capturing the hearts of the fair ladies that populate this site like dandelions in green fields.

I must also remark that it is the dark cloud, I believe, whose lining is rumored to be silver. Perhaps that is not the idiom exactly, but I picture it to be part and parcel, as that saying goes, with its intended meaning. So, beware the darkness, too! (Though every yearning Heathcliff is a worthy man and worthy lover, at best.)

As you can tell and guess, I am quite educated, capable, at any rate, of spinning a fine sentence — thus revealing good schooling and good intellect — and also capable of a playful self-mockery, even to a perfect stranger whom I am seeking to woo.

If you believe we have "the common thread" you speak of, and find me to be more Theseus than Minotaur, send me a sign of your interest, and we shall have sandwiches and coffee, by the dog of Egypt, anon.

Thine,

Egbert

Dear Caroline8,

Finally, someone's pulled the wool off Manhattan. Now I'm the poor son who's lost his father's blessing. Will you cloak me, cover me, pull some sort of coat over me? I'm cold, tired, and thirsty. For a cup of coffee, a crust of advice, a little something to take the edge off my winter.

Egbert

Hi, Oceanlife,

I actually grew up on the water sailing. While it's been a few years since I've been out on a sailboat, it's a feeling that never leaves you.

Here on Match.com, to tell you the truth, I feel like I keep putting notes in bottles. They all go out to sea, and never come back.

Still, I haven't given up. I hope you read this, write me a note, and toss the bottle back. If you do, we can talk about Henry James, whom I am re-reading actually right now, and other things.

I'll wait on the beach for a little while.

Egbert

Cindy ("Oceanlife")

Cindy was a widow, and the last time I had been to the Botanic Gardens was when my son was three, and I thought seeing the cherry trees blossoming would be a beautiful thing to do together with her. There was, as we spied each other from across the corners on 2nd Avenue at East 83rd Street, the signs of mutual recognition, which means a flash of joy in spotting who we were the first time we met; and I, for one, because of this, did not put much stock in Cindy's relational parameters.

Her point of view, which she had established in our email correspondence that went back sporadically a couple of months, was that our not becoming romantic would "avoid future pain." While it was true and obvious that I lived a hundred miles north of her, this I saw as a localized ploy to fend off a more global fear of beginning any relationship that might, if it were meaningful, carry with it grief's inherency of potential loss, a fact that was plainly part of Cindy's personal history; and I, given her admiration for me, based solely on our emails, could perhaps be, or become, such a person in her life.

Getting to Brooklyn from the Upper East Side took forever, and even though I got lost driving there, neither she nor I was vexed. Where neither criticism is deployed for my getting the way all screwed up, nor my feeling criticized for the same felt, these, too, are good signs for the beginning of any relationship. Standing in line on an early Saturday afternoon in April to buy tickets, we no doubt looked like spring lovers, as did the many others who seemed to me equally lovestruck.

You would not have guessed that we had just seen each other one hour prior for the first time. I stood close to her, and she stood close to me. While I did not hold her hand or arm, an occasional grazing touch from me to her would have made on onlooker think that we were no doubt intimate.

Nevertheless, I could see that Cindy and I had different eyes for wonder as well as politics. Me, I am mesmerized by the giant carp that one sees lolling about in the pond, grotesque and beautiful. Cindy barely wanted to glimpse. Maybe it was due to the packs of families overlooking these monstrous-looking fishes that put her off, and the fact that Cindy had neither a husband nor children. Who could say? And, as our conversation wandered somehow into the Dalai Lama, she wanted to know why I liked him. The question was put to me critically, and I ended up feeling a little defensive of him before a woman I was still trying to woo. These two sentiments were incompatible, so I let his Holiness slide.

There was one picture that both Cindy and I took along the trail, she on her phone and me on my digital camera. I'd brought the latter just in case we'd hit it off and I'd wanted something to remember her by. There was a tree; I believe it was an American Sycamore. Its bark was carved up and down and all around the trunk, as high as a knife in hand could reach, and as low to the dirt as letters could go, spelling out couples' now anonymous initials.

She took it, and so did I, but we did not take a photograph on this trip through the garden of each other for memory's sake, where the cherry blossoms were just beginning to open, or any other, where we had come a week or two prematurely, before the full bloom, before the full warmth of spring had actually hit.

CHAPTER EIGHT: GLORIA ("wastedhatwix")

LETTERS:

Dear Mingming114

Hi, Posey

Hi, Ckl2cldkny

Dear Springbreeze

Hi, Kindawarmbright

Yo, CSommerville

Hi, Joycouldbeours

Hi, Kcm917

Dearest Chrysalis

Dear wastedhatwix

STORY: Gloria ("wastedhatwix")

Dear Mingming114,

I have come to visit you two or three times. I thought you were a very cute animal, one that I would like to take home with me. The first time I came and poked my finger through your cage, you licked it. I thought it meant you liked me, that you wanted to leave that dirty "shelter" of yours.

When I came back the next day, you were either asleep or just chose to ignore me. Now, I know that animals who have been abandoned by their keepers can be that way. I know they can be temperamental and moody. I know that rescue animals often have these sorts of trust issues, and that it takes time.

Sometimes, when an animal has lived in a shelter too long, it gets too comfortable there, and becomes afraid to come out, even into the sunshine, even when there is a kind hand, even when there might be a warm home for it. They get used to a bad situation that they know, and become afraid to try a new one that is unknown, even if it might be better.

I came back one more time. I looked at you with kind eyes. I saw that you were very pretty. I felt that you were lonely there in your cage, day and night. I noticed, too, how you stirred and looked out longingly from your cage very, very early in the morning, and often late at night, too. Seeing you move about in the darkness like that made me feel affection and longing for you.

I am here at the animal shelter one more time; it might be the last. If you make even a little yelp, give the slightest oink, or make the softest purr, I promise you I'll come back again.

Just stir a little, make only a little noise, and I'll come back as often as you need, again and again, before you feel comfortable enough for me to open up the door to your cage and come out of the old familiar safety of it into the new fresh open world with me.

Egbert

Hi, Posey,

You look and sound so sweet; I wish I could hire a troop of bodyguards just to protect you. I always think beautiful girls like you are going to fall like grapes into the wrong mouth, especially when, as you say, English is not your first language.

Be careful! You have been so open and honest in your profile here, but mark my word: many are the false princes who will seek and flatter you, who, in retrospect, you will have been luckier to have kissed a poison toad.

If I'm wrong in this, and you really are a good listener, as you say, then I'm glad; for it means you already do know how to choose a partner and best protect yourself by hearing the intentions of others — both good and not — for what and who they really are.

Egbert

Hi, Ckl2cldkny:

I've never had a practical kind of *realpolitik* relationship to both parties' mutual advantage before, but I couldn't help noticing that you are an editor and a writer, as you say "by trade." I could use a person with a good brain, a good ear, and a good pen with the heart of Ms. Theresa and the pluck of Mr. Jones to listen to my texts and get them to the right places and desks. To risk immodesty, no, to be flat-out immodest: I will be the find of your life, that way. In return, my prodigious powers will be backed by prodigious, ample, fair stores of regenerative warmth and kindness that will bathe you in comfort, swaddle you in laughter, and protect you, to the extent that I can, from idle swarms of locusts, clouds of gnats, and small groups of evil-doers.

Yours,

Egbert

Dear Springbreeze,

You are the very first person in over 500 profiles, probably a 1000, to say either of these two things: I've got great calves and I'm a passionate lover. With your net cast over 5000 miles, you've probably got every devil-fish with a working dorsal fin after you for that one. Do you want fire? I have got bundles of it. Do want the stats to back it up, no, that's sort of off-putting. Besides, we're both educated people; and, after all, I'm the writerly, intellectual type. But, I confess, I am in top physical shape. I am lean and toned and my blood-pumping heart will not give out on you at night. I'll squeeze those proud calves of yours and make you giggle; quote Li Po, but never drown smiling in the liquor of my smile; I'll make you late for work, and happily use up that extra two weeks of vacation.

Egbert

Hi, Kindawarmbright,

I'm afraid the last thing I am is well-rounded. I do play piano, classical. I do ski, downhill. I do garden, organic. I do recycle: glass, paper, and metal. I do read, literature. Do these things make me well-rounded? I once wished to be that; it was a failure. I basically realized in my early twenties that I was good for nothing except one thing, writing. I really couldn't do anything else. In everything else, I was pretty much useless. *El Inútil.* But I do remember and remember it fondly, quite fondly, banging the shuttlecocks over the slumping net on our side lawn where we avoided stepping into the soggy spot where the septic tank was. Yes, that was home, good Greenwich, the one and only, that pushed me to excellence, rocket high SAT's, a smackin' IQ, and a nostalgia for rhododendrons, pachysandra, and ovenbirds that flew to their deaths in plate glass windows, and trust funds that washed out off the rocky beach at the end of the road to lawyers elsewhere in Long Island, perhaps.

Yes, yes, I've always had confidence and energy, the fine things you speak of, so much so I've had to toss it away to the *clochards* in Paris who were, by definition, homeless and sometime shoeless as well. And as for my attractiveness, as one of the two still living East Indian bald homosexual twins from Boston who ran the American Café in Amsterdam said to me, before fobbing me off for the night to have sex with some good-hearted girl on the pill way back in the 80's, "You're not a beauty, but you've got something!"

yrs.,

Egbert

Yo, CSommerville,

I'm a guy with nuthin gowin fer him. I figur a blund chick like yo'd like to kick it sum up with me cuz I'm real, eef you know whut Im' sayin; like i gotta trust fun frum newton's where my hommies iz i'd like to share up with you and doo it up rite together with yoo sum time cuz i like yoo i kin jus tell it like you no it.

Egbert

Hi, Joycouldbeours:

The "addiction" to online dating you mention in your profile is probably just an obsession to nothing that actually works! How many times have I come home from work, and checked my email to see if anyone's emailed me from Match? And usually there's nothing, nothing at all. And how many times have I read a woman's profile, drunk it in, like a fine glass of Tokay wine, become just ever so slightly inspired and delirious from it, written her a note that varies in degree of fun and seriousness, only to find myself no better off than my having tossed corked bottles with absolutely NOTHING in them at all into the Pacific? I couldn't count. So, the addiction, like now with you, if it is one, is an addiction to hope — that someone is bright enough, and funny enough, and open enough, and basically just real enough to write me back, go out with me (after the obligatory email exchanges wherein we both try to discover that the other person is safe), and take it from there.

Here goes another bottle!

yrs.,

Egbert

Hi, Kcm917,

It sounds like you've figured out something about this site that too many people seem to miss: instead of it being just a hit-or-miss "booty call" spot, or the place to get off on whatever fetish you've got, and we all do have them, to one degree or another, you can actually connect with people you never would. You can open up parts of yourself that would otherwise be stifled, shut down, dormant.

As John Berryman wrote, "After all, the sky flashes, the great sea yearns, we ourselves flash and yearn," which, more than anything is about a call to connect with people, with, as you wrote, "someone who will entertain me and make me laugh till i have to pee"; it's really the same thing, even if one's a couple of lines of poetry and the other's just a casual, off-the-cuff desire.

The truth is, it is hard to find people with whom you will LET yourself go so completely that you will just sit there and pee in your pants practically. And, in fact, it's probably never going to be that tall dark stranger you said you don't want bugging you who's generally going to be half in love with his own shadow more than he is with you anyway! So, good riddance, pal!

"Genuine people," the kind you want, they screw up, they mess up, they are attentive and caring, they listen to you, they tell you when you look good, they tell you when you look like shit, they swear, they're vulgar, they're polite, they know how to treat waitstaff well, they know how to tell you "no" when your shit is coming up in their faces, they are forgiving and mean it, they apologize and mean it, they write in run-on sentences and make total sense, and can also turn a phrase that's lofty, precise, and elegant; they're hopeful and do feel longing, they're hopeless and do feel despair, they're realistic and know when the gig's up, they remember your number because they fall in love with you, they delete your number when you tell them it's over.

Write me back, if you'd like; maybe we'll get a little back and forth going, and maybe down the road we'll find each other at some joint with sawdust on the floor and a porter-house in front of us.

Egbert

Dearest Chrysalis:

My first wife went to Brown.

My second wife went to Columbia.

The first girl I slept with went to Yale.

The last one went to Harvard.

My brother went to Princeton.

My sister went to Amherst.

My son goes to Wesleyan.

But I went to Middlebury.

Except for maybe my son, I'm smarter than them all.

Do you think I have a chance?

Egbert

Dear wastedhatwix,

You might be everything you say you are; in that case, we just might be able to do something. Abnormal, simply away from the middle 2/3's of the slush pile. And I am way, way out there, about three standard deviations; you pick which side. But, so far on this infernal site — besides one door-pounding PhD maniac and one borderline, it's all fizzle. Just a bunch of half-dreamers who've got some half-assed persona they're not even half a continent close to living, let alone being able to fake it for an hour in person. And believe me, I've tried.

You might just be the real thing. I've had a lot of fun doing the searches under the usual words that were funny "Ivy," "slut," "biped," "smart," "creative," — stuff I tend to like, and plugged in "genius." Finally, right, I got honest. Should I have tried "humble" or "enlightened" or "funny when hit by lightning"? Fuck if I know.

You claim you like tenacious people. Tenacious? Addictive? Obsessive? You have no idea. I'll tell you why I do it: everything I do gets chewed up and spat back out as art. You, too; right now. This is my book. You are my book. Does that entice you? Do you want to see my book? See your place in it? I touch a thing; it becomes brilliant; I think a thing; it is. Megalomaniac? Only to tempt you towards me, but not. Sociopath: not. Dangerous: could be, have been. 'Member, you're the one who claims she bites, not I. (I'll remember that, and blame myself later.)

You're wrong: more than 50% change is for the worse. About 99.9% is always for the worse. To do any good, you've got to be that last little percentage. The rest is just the seaweed and crap that rolls up on the shore. But, hell, every beach needs its mound of pretension and desire.

Rebelling for the sake of rebelling, which you bring up, is just dumb. Reread your Kant about that under Genius — of all things! Of course you're just scared to shit that you're really just sorta average, after all, and might even just chew off the hand that feeds you just to prove for a weekend in hell that you're not.

Face it: you're another sodden brilliant romantic, like me, who's fucking yearning for the real thing, not just some jackass water-based paint job that'll peel off your third step put on by the jackass who put it there.

I don't need to go anywhere or do anything. Skip the travel. Skip the this. Skip the that. (But mind the dentist.) I make up (and write down) one world after the next. And you're part of it now.

Know a genius; write me; stop screwing around.

Egbert

Gloria ("wastedhatwix")

Before driving hours in the middle of the night right to Gloria's house, after emailing her, IMing each other, and then talking on the phone, she wanted to be sure I knew she was bipolar, fat, and smoked pot. I did. I knew. And I set off already dead tired following my Google Maps directions to what were the netherlands of New Jersey, hours and hours from home at two o'clock in the morning.

Her big house in the dark woods was filled with all sorts of bric-a-brac, the sort of pseudo-60's psychedelia that belonged either to a washed-out throwback or a fuck-it-I-like-it person who's brutally sure of themselves, their tastes, what they like. Gloria was 29 years old, not the 60's.

I was so exhausted I soon ended up in her bed, just to lie there. It was the place to talk. She kissed me a little, but I wasn't into it. She was just too big, and I was scared anyway. I mean, it would have been weird for me to have sex with a really large Chinese woman. It would certainly have been a first for me. But, in addition to that, and my exhaustion, the entire trip felt as though I were in an intellectual headlock with someone no less fond of being put in one herself.

Gloria had the home court advantage and I had nowhere else to go. It was like a fiendish story I'd read years back by Pär Lagerkvist about a fat farmer's wife who seduced a man who later, having run past his wits' end, jumped into the revolving millwheel the next morning while toothlessly, her arms folded over her fat breasts like loaves, she and her husband above the roar and the din of the millwheel turning from the water and the force of the stream, watched with mirth and laughter as the man was bashed to death by the wooden paddles of the turning millwheel.

After my drive, I saw there was nowhere else to go. I had been physically too exhausted to move. But I was conscious enough to feel that if something went wrong, I was a dead man. So, the last thing that I could let happen was for my pants to be off. For surely, if I were not aroused by Gloria, I had to be prepared to die.

My paranoia abated when I left her bed, following her suggestion, to sleep on a twin mattress in the guest room. When the next day came, I had to stay. I could not just run. That was still too dangerous. I had to create the aura of my feeling comfortable.

I learned, while I drank orange juice and she got high, that Gloria had not changed her house a bit since her divorce had been finalized. The dishes in the sink hadn't been washed in long time. She told me to guess when. I figured two weeks, three. It was a year ago, she let me know.

I didn't feel she was either lugubrious or stuck. She actually had a kind of psychotic brilliance, and she was disappointed with my own. She'd expected a much edgier, aggressive, incandescent man. When I feel threatened, however, I tend to get calm and almost easygoing. I adopt a sort of homespun, offhand demeanor that belies my fear. This way I don't threaten my enemy, which of course is the point. I don't endanger myself, and adopt a mien that lets me see full circle what is going on around me. I do not climb into a fox hole.

She cried, wept, when she started washing her dishes. It was a start, and we both knew it.

I thought Gloria was going to smash my computer when she caught a glimpse of one of the women I was pursuing on Match. I had brought her into the ongoings of my Match project, but had tried to keep the screen from her view. When she saw the woman I was pining for was Asian, that was it. Gloria grew red and furious. She talked about how she was seen as ugly by Chinese. She wanted to know what was my thing with Chinese. My back was against the wall. Now, I was going to die.

To my surprise, she summed up my explanation as aesthetic and intellectual. Her fury, her potential wrath, was centered on the notion of men wanting the little docile submissive Asian female which she was not. She had turned her entire physical being against this stereotype. I felt spared. I felt lucky.

When we talked about my project, though Gloria was not dazzled by my idea to make a book out of all my Match letters, she thought it made sense. She was involved in a project, too, one that required daily upkeep of her profile, changes she made to it, and a coterie of men who used it almost like a private service. She wanted to develop programs, using algorithms, to make the whole thing interactive. As a computer programmer, she wanted to apply to Match math the way I had applied to it words.

We had some sympathetic overlaps. Pot, alcohol, a bottle of meds, and an atomizer next to her couch in the solarium made Gloria's home seem like a place where wrong things could easily happen, where they could go bad fast. She was attracted to my claim in my first email of being three standard deviations out there. I'm sure she really was.

When I gave her a hug goodbye, and felt her body against mine a moment, I felt like Odysseus having escaped Circe's hut, only more narrowly: he had help and outside information and shipmates; I was in the deep woods of New Jersey on my own with a silver car.

CHAPTER NINE: Meiling ("Rathertimely")

LETTERS:

Dear Marynyc

Dear Sakura

Hi, Greenonion

Dear Djdcgurl

Well, Belle

Dear Parfois [1]

Dear Parfois [2]

Dear Grtchn1981

Dear Loveintegration

Dear MyPicasso

Dear Rathertimely

STORY: Meiling ("Rathertimely")

Dear Marynyc:

Yes, you're right: people can write anything here, and I'm beginning to have my doubts about what people say. I'm not sure if people even mean to make things up, but I don't really think people want the things they claim they want. Sure, it's easy to say that you want someone who is worldly, funny, smart, handsome, gentle, direct, honest, and all that. But if that were truly the case I'd have a lot more replies than I do. Of course, why take my word for it, anymore than I take the word of people I never hear back from who say they want... well, you know what they want. Oh, brother!

You're right: if you want to get a sense of someone, see the person in person. If you think you'd like to know me, for instance, send me a line, and let me know.

Egbert

Dear Sakura,

It's strange that a hedonistic little go-getter such as yourself should cross that Austrian billionaire off your list. After all, with so many children and so much money, you know the dude was good for something. I mean, for that bitch-goddess of a governess to stick with him, he had to have given her something real good. And those other fellas you mention on the silver screen, they're all just different shades of the same kind of plastic puppetry, in my opinion. Don't get me wrong: I'm not espousing, as it were, a roll in the hay with a Kaiser von Somebody. I am no Prince Neo, nor was meant to be, but I'm no attendant lord either. I myself am more the Prince Hamlet type: vain, sexy, overinvolved, overstimulated, deeper and more intelligent than is generally good for the usual posy-ringed girl to deal with. But, you're a Wall Streeter. You're smart. I bet we could cuddle up one afternoon when you ditch your job and I ditch mine and read verses of Lao Tzu in soft white sheets together, and teach each other like children learning to smile; and then, in our afternoon sleep, we may for a spell return to being the perfect blocks of woods we once were and originally are, as the text goes.

Egbert

Hi, Greenonion:

I have combed this site like a kid who's lost his favorite color crayon somewhere at his friend's house, and your oddly third person profile definitely takes the cake for being fun, provocative, and jaw-dropping. With your ear muffs in the summer, footstomps on pigeons, spoof on Asian-girl stereotype, and tummy-bared come-ons to the yearning romanticism lurking in the heart and groin of every man who can lift a shaker of salt over his fries, your totally wild-ass play is irresistible.

"Lucky to have you"? Honey, are you kidding me? You are the type of woman men kill themselves for. You're Dante's Beatrice. John Donne's Anne. Humbert Humbert's lovebug. Sappho's cliff dive. Joyce's Nora. You are the top button of every woman's blouse, undone, undoing. Men forget their wives, children, families, jobs, careers, continents just to feel your breath near theirs. Your chronic "headache" and 24/7 "madness" would be well worth the bargain to have you in my life.

Egbert

Dear Djdcgurl:

With that camera in hand and your belly button showing, I bet every wacko this side of the Mississippi has filled your mailbox with all sorts of obnoxious stuff. But, truth be told, your perspective is practical and dead on: how on earth can anybody claim to strike it big with love before you know if you can even have fun together? What a breath of fresh air, really, your profile is, a breath of honest fresh air. Of course, you're the girl, and you get to pick and choose. Lucky you!

Egbert

Well, Belle:

You spurned me once, but I don't care. I'm still in this devil-of-a-meat-market, and so are you, I noticed. Doesn't make any sense to me either. I know, you're the humble and softly ironic sort who minimizes her own intelligence by disavowing what her own friends say about her by suggesting that she really is not that bright; and me, I'm really just a pompous dolt. Which explains why neither of us has really gotten anywhere on this site. Right? Wrong.

I'm not trying to skate on your pond just for sex; I got the message, actually, in your profile: your ice is a little thin, and you don't want to be trampled on. And if you are, the guy's going to fall into the freezing cold water with you. Then comes the mammalian diving reflex, and it's all history. The old, "As two spent swimmers do drown together and choke their art."

If we ever do actually go out together some evening, you know, after we've traded emails and a couple of secrets and stuff like that, let's go to some restaurant in the Meatpacking District; it'd be fitting, funny, fun, and altogether cute.

Egbert

Dear Parfois,

Christ! You are a fresh blot of light in this sea of perpetual darkness. And while it's so late at night that the dog of Egypt is beginning to howl, I'm just going to have to make a new cup of coffee to write you a note that I hope you can make believe you found pinned to the corner of your mattress by your well-skinned knees in the morning, or anytime around noon when you pull your body out of bed from its slumber.

While it seems that this whole Match-site is set up like a flea market where everyone from Yemen to Massachusetts is standing in line to get their rings properly sized, the whole beauty of it is almost entirely missed. It's really an autonomous playground of fantasies and photos where our best personal fictions can be interwoven with Scheherazade's dusky lovers. One or two people out of almost a hundred so far, besides you, get this.

A line like, "I don't intend to sell stock on a dating site therefore don't see the point in spelling myself out to the world," is so brilliant, I don't know why a thousand young gentleman have not pulled their letter openers out of their books, and thrust the points of them into their hearts for you. I would. And yet, I am still awaiting the return flight of Saint-Exupéry, and must warn him of the simoom I fear will take down his small aircraft just over the next sandcrest. I would. And yet, I am awaiting the lanterns of Arabia to close their eyes, and for the stars overhead to hold in their nocturnal gazes the agonies of the sleeping until the morrow, when work and toil and pointless fig-tossing renews itself, as always. I would myself, except it is I now who follows you, Eurydice, a poor, barefoot, broken-stringed Orpheus who will disappear forever the moment you look at him instead. So, bury me.

Egbert

Dear Parfois,

Before I get going, and I will get going, I do wish to repeat an earlier sentiment that I believe I expressed about your profile; and if not, not exactly, will now. Of the now hundreds and hundreds of women's profiles that I have scanned & read, and of the couple hundred I've hunkered down to respond to, yours remains one of the best.

While I am preaching to the choir, allow me for a moment to lapse into that cliché in order to establish at least an e-semblance of common ground. Using this site as a hitching post for mutual booty is, while desirable, to squander its very usefulness through such narrowly defined limits. As you wrote when you lapsed into the warm spot of sincerity in your profile that you'd "like to meet quality people that I can learn from, share stories and experiences with, and perhaps exchange a solid friendship with," that, in its broader sense, is a far more, dare I say, evolved perspective.

And it is in this regard that I can say I have been pretty successful so far. I have definitely met people with top-notch minds and world perspectives unlike, but mostly still compatible, with my own. Moreover, and perhaps more importantly, I have been able to watch how I myself change, evolve, process, deal with, and manage the different situations in both cyber-life and sidewalk-life that I have encountered here or as a result of Match.

For example, without going into the sawdust and details, I have been on actual dates with inconsiderate women who pick their teeth, make numerous cellphone calls, and are generally rude throughout a lunch date; but, even while there is not even a thanks for my taking them out, what I learn is that I am, in fact, a gentleman. Sure, it's easy to be polite and kind and charming when I'm sitting across from a beautiful, well-educated, self-aware person. But the test of who I am really comes when I follow through with a commitment

I have made to spend my time with someone whom I can see, right off the bat, has not had the many advantages that I have had in life; and, as a result, lacks both the grace and poise that comes easily and naturally to me. Then, how do I as a human being behave? Then, how do I as a human being treat who is, when you get right down to it, another human being? And how I do that is all important. In the end, it is simply my being a decent person. We will all, and we all do have, dealings with goods and money and people and relationships and items — all the stuff of the world; but HOW we do this is what makes an actual difference.

I have also had brilliant and gorgeous, highly successful Harvard PhD's, whom I have called a mutually accepted end to a relationship with, beating at my front door two Fridays later. And it is here that I learn the painful lesson of not allowing, in spite of a person's obvious intelligence and appeal in many ways, another's personal issues to overtake me, by locking my door before her and drawing that physical barrier between us, knowing, of course that I am not only protecting myself, but that my doing this is also for her own good.

I have exchanged notes with people who are mystical, whose depth and insight draw me to know them and how they view the world better.

I have met fellow travelers whose bumps and bruises feel akin to my own; and feel that I have collected, perhaps, here, of all places, a new genuine friend for life.

I have watched my own heart and mind open up in many unexpected, unknown places; and, while many, if not most, of these encounters are fleeting, they all change me. That, really, is the point: to do things in life that continue to change me. In that way, of course, I continue to become.

So, I like how you put it that you're not selling stock here; it isn't an IPO, exactly. No, you like me, in your way, have done (or do) an initial screening through this site, either with your profile or the responses you get from it. Mine, as it is written, only attracts a certain crowd, if you will, of people. I won't spell 'em out with adjectives. I, like you, am not selling myself to the public. If I were, believe me, I'd do it completely differently. You, on the other hand, go about it by spoofing the Asian Girl image, in essence, by first projecting that in your initial image — the elegant, made up perfectly, almond-eyed beauty thing and all that — and then go on to twist the panties off nearly every rice-dick reading your profile — whether the jerk-off gets it or not. It's simply a different way of screening, but, I think, with or toward the same result: seeking quality people.

And that is where the "crazy and small world" you write of becomes exciting, I think. In a way, it might be something like the Temporary Autonomous Zone that the thinker and writer Hakim Bey writes about, and which I admire. Look him up if you're not familiar with his writings. The vanity and misfortune that can occur is the mistaken and false notion that you or I are the only smart and aware and feeling and deep people in the world; or, that there are few of us; or, that we are a "dying breed." All that is true vanity. And it is simply, and thankfully, not true at all! We are many, and this putative schtupping site has revealed how many there are of us in the world to me.

Egbert

Dear Grtchn1981:

There is no art to your profile. You could be the next Jane Austen and probably are. But there's still no art to your profile. You could be the next Willa Cather. And might be. Yet the simple, straightforward plainness of attributes that you lay out to define yourself to your reader have almost no picture to them. I was first struck by this when I saw your primary photograph a day or so ago. You appeared, because of the pink hue to your dress, to be, in juxtaposition to the light color of your skin, naked; yet, because of the dress material covering your body, breastless. That would make you a kind, not a cruel, Lady Macbeth who has unsexed herself.

It could just be that you are just comfortable being in your own skin. No one who wasn't would list having a salamander as their favorite animal. (I happen to be fond of them myself; the woods and forest I live in, beneath the rocks, are sleeping with bright orange efts and others.) No one else would list as a merit her being a truly sucky piano player. (I, too, happen to have taught myself well enough to play some easy Beethoven sonatas, some delightful Mozart, and some of Bach's easier Goldberg Variations on my piano.) No one else would admit to being both valedictorian — apparently twice — and a reader of the Harry Potter series. (OK, I wasn't ranked as highly as you, either time; and I made it through, I believe, 4 1/2 books of HP; but, I have read Homer, have studied Classical Greek, and am into both classical rock and, as indicated above, classical music as well.)

I am not, among other things you want, blond and blue-eyed. Like you, however, I am nominally Jewish. I do hope that you really are, as you say, someone who "could be up for anything," the "could" being the fulcrum upon which all pivots.

You don't, by the way, sound corny. You sound simply as though you are opening up; maybe you'll show me what that is like a little bit, and I'll show you, too.

Egbert

Dear Loveintegration,

I have a total e-crush on you. I saw your picture and starting reading your profile, and it was uh-oh all the way through. I love how you write, how your mind is thinking and smiling in and out here. I wish I were across from you at some little wooden table and it's my guess, hope, desire, and belief that you'd get me; you'd see me nodding *yes* to all the things that matter. And I am totally botching it here, whipping through this note without barely thinking (even though I refused to write you last night when I stumbled across your profile, saving it for when I'd be composed and clear and articulate) rather than fumbling around like this.

yrs.,

Egbert

Dear MyPicasso,

The way I look at it is there's the risk of crowding you in or full disclosure that just leaves me open. And, there's little time, little space between the two. And, if I'm gotten, I'm gotten; and if not, not. While it's totally and certainly un-Matchlike to unbuckle one's armor of anonymity, I don't feel like leaving question marks hovering like umbrellas in your mind about me; rather, I'd prefer they crashed into the ground point-first, or that you and I should promenade together down the red-stone concourse of a resort I once knew in Monastir, Tunisia, parasol in hand, my arm crooked, and your hand upon my forearm, many years ago, when I was a boy the first time I ever fell in love, and flirted unknowingly with two polite French homosexuals vacationing there.

Ah, Sunflower, you ask for passion, and, fun, and scarysmart, if possible. And I am hiding in the cornfield, I am hiding behind some Gansevoort slaughterhouse, I am appearing like a blind spot, sunspot in your rearview mirror; I am scrubbing the soap stains from your bathtub away, I am pressing my thumbs against the balls of your feet, I am planting my palms upon your shoulder blades, I am playing a little Goldberg, a variation or two, I am reading Gödel Escher Bach, I am singing the Eensy-Weensy Spider, I am faking accents of people I've never known, I am yelling obscenities at my reflection in a passing mirror, I am the cut of a gentleman in my suit, I am the picture of a hick in my overalls, I am more arrogant than Thomas Jefferson on Whitsunday, I am as humble as Horatio watching his friend about to die, I am stable as a keel, mad as a hatter, as brilliant as magnesium burning, as wild and romantic as laudanum-infused Coleridge, as delirious and self-obsessed and sex-possessed as Schiele before being wiped out by influenza; as patient as ooze, as hopeful as Castro, as dangerous as the nocturnal fisher, as devoted as a crucifix, as ridiculous and as sublime as the two peacocks that used to strut the grounds opposite the Hungarian Cafe and scrape their tails on Amsterdam, as poetic and determined as Menander on a good day, Homer on a bad; I am the swan of Tuonela; Caravaggio on his own; Paganini, Nijinsky in his journals, Pieter Peeperkorn declaiming under the waterfalls; I am the childhood animal in *Put Me in the Zoo* who plays with colored spots, I am the rose the Little Prince almost forgot.

Egbert

Dear Rathertimely:

You are mesmerizing.

Nobody leaves me at a loss for words; you have. So, I'm just going to dig some pieces out of a few novels of mine for you to read. These are in answer to your thoughts about having a "sharp mind," "a light, joyous and playful heart," and a "tough stomach." (I want to talk to you about parenthood [see Thomas Bernhard in *Gathering Evidence* on it, brilliant, like your take], and middle age ["I'll never never get to that"], and children themselves ["like seagulls to breakwater rocks they come to me"], and everything else we will ever think of.

Your profile is a fresh simoom of joy and delight blown in over all the drek of middle-nothing desires and middle-nothing values here and elsewhere I've never had and never aspired to. Write me back; if you don't, what a disaster for both of us, a total all-out loss.

I hope to meet you soon.

Egbert

Meiling ("rathertimely")

I'd maintained for years that Dia, a former Nabisco box-printing factory now gargantuan art museum, would be the perfect place to break up with somebody. The voluminous building housing the works of Donald Judd, John Chamberlain, Andy Warhol, and Fred Sandback gave ample room to amble and, during a difficult and tight conversation with someone, space to move away from them, while continuing that private conversation. And, too, since it was public, no conversation could get that out of hand. To me, and I have been there with several women, girlfriends and not, it was the ideal nexus between private and public.

Because Meiling lived somewhere in New Jersey that I have never been, and, given her Amy Winehouse and intellectual proclivities, I suggested via email that we meet there, the midway point between our two homes. When we met, I discarded that she looked neither as young and sassy as her online pictures portrayed her as, but had a harder time with her oversized designer sunglasses that looked like they'd been snatched in a mall or found on the counter in a nail salon, an odd look for an earth-cracking rebel-girl, I thought. At any rate, they were only sunglasses, and few of us look as good in person as the photos we post.

We toured the museum with nods and pointings, and had similar tastes of what worked and what did not. There was an aesthetic overlap of 86-92%. And that's not bad. Especially for the first time.

Instead of pushing her back against the steel plates of Richard Serra and kissing her, I told her about my urge to do so. Nor would she execute the same fantasy upon me. In fact, she was surprised at how polite I was. She'd expected, evidently, someone more outrageous. I had, however, told her in an email, that the one thing I could promise her when we met was safety.

I was not troubled in the least that Meiling criticized my work. I'm sure some very bright people criticized Picasso's so-called Blue Period work. And I'm sure there are well-meaning, intelligent people who criticize the stupendous work of Anselm Kiefer. I myself am well-familiar with the taking exception to of story-telling, story-writing, story-making altogether. From punk-ass intellectuals decrying it, to the great Kenzaburo Oe disavowing it, the art of making fiction is to some a debatable or even worthless undertaking. I don't mind; it is what I do; I aim to do it better, as I always have. I suppose you could break it down into a couple of camps — the Thomas Bernhard types who swear on the promised and damned grave of Austria that they lie but their intention is to tell the truth; and others who dismiss this leg of the noble triad, thus crippling the others, Beauty and the Good, and thereby the entire beast collapses. From Derrida to Paul de Man to Christopher Norris and Nehamas and back, we could go on and on; and I'd just return to the *Protagoras*, for one, and the famous *pharmakon*, for two, and begin there with Plato in Attic Greek, driven as I am, always to text, the original, autochthonous, chthonic underworld of the written word itself where raped Persephone trades beads of sweat for the blood of a pomegranate.

I was hardly impressed, then, when after I'd asked Meiling where she'd learned to think the way she did she said, "Nietzsche." It was the big Oh-No in my vocabulary, the one where I hear the difference between a reader who confuses being radical with being an individual, between being an upstart and a thinker, between narcissism and work.

Still, as we roamed the sheet metal strips of one installation, the sand piles of the next, plywood boxes of another, and floor-to-ceilings threads of a fourth, I did not wholly give up on Meiling. She did have an eye; she did have a mind; she was attractive enough; we admired much of what we saw the same. If only she'd shake off her seriousness, she might be fun, I had hoped, thinking the brass ring of Louise Bourgeois' penises might do it. No luck. And if penises on a coffee table, if big cocks hanging overhead in your mouth can't make you smile, little I feel can.

Still thinking we had a lot more to talk about, since we'd only been there about an hour, I proposed once the museum had closed, that we go somewhere else, like a coffee shop in Beacon. Meiling suggested my house. Once there, an hour away, a good four for her now from her own New Jersey home, she confessed that she had wanted to meet me to shake from me my image of her. She also confessed to not being physically attracted to me. At my house. Which she had suggested coming to. An hour away. She called it chemistry.

Maybe if we screwed, it'd make a difference. She'd open up. I mumbled something, some kind of ridiculous and manipulative nonsense as she stood at my front door with the keys to her minivan in hand, and kissed her cheek because she'd turned her mouth. That was a mistake, not a bad one on my part, and I knew it. But I didn't care either that much. She wasn't really that sexy to begin with, and she wasn't very sexy at that point at all for sure, but I was a little pissed off. A little bit tantalized, you might say. Or blue balled you could also. Or just dicked around by this nobody. Yup, I was angry. She had denied my longing where she felt none. I had held her close to me in my house. That part she accepted. She had felt nice. Christ! When she was going, I just wanted to break the ice.

CHAPTER TEN: XO ("Cometochina")

LETTERS:

Dear Keelimepie

Dear Onlyorganic

Dear Ermoose

Hi, not2spookie

Hi, Snow38

Dear Asiangrl75

Hi, Roseyfuture222

Dear Everlucky

Dear Firehouse5

Dear Moviemiss

Dude, aka AMd511

Dear Editor

Hi, Cometochina

STORY: Xo ("Cometochina")

Dear Keelimepie

I'm so "comfortable in my skin," as you like your men to be, that I never take mine off. It has, in truth, just as many hair follicles as a chimpanzee's hide, but the bulk of these are inactive. Still, I like to keep it clean, and wash it at least once a day with either a lye-based or an olive oil-based soap. My epidermis is pretty blanched, as far as skins go, being a mixture mostly of potato-eating people from the Hebrides and homeless Semites who wandered around the Urals possibly ages ago. Over the years, I have had a number of small accidents that have resulted in my skin being cut open in several different places, but these were easily repaired, and, except with the closest and most intimate of inspections, you'd hardly notice. All in all, I am enjoying being what the Buddhist monks refer to as a dung sack on stilts. I'm not sure what your own skin is like or how comfortable you are in it, but if you feel as though you might like mine, if its texture or its hue appears pleasing to you, write me a note with your fingers, and perhaps some day we will see what we are like to each other with most of our skins covered up.

Egbert

Dear Onlyorganic,

No offense, but how anybody could read John Updike is beyond me. I read 2,000 pages of him when I was stuck in Budapest in 1985, and he is without a doubt the least interesting most plodding least inspirational most insipid "writer" I have ever come across. Not a grain of poetry in him. No magic. Dull as the backside of a dartboard.

Yours,

Egbert

Dear Ermoose:

It's hard to tell whether or not you've had the despotic joy of waking up with somebody who rolls over and checks out what's new going on on Match. You know, somebody who's better-looking, smarter, taller, younger, sexier, and promises a better and more stable future. So, sure, I get your urge to end this whole thing. But, it's not so easy, is it? After all, if you do meet somebody, it's a bit forceful for either to insist that the other quit Match, isn't it? There's virtually no history behind the two of them; so, the idea of deleting Match is akin to forcing someone to quit a magazine subscription you yourself don't approve of — which is problematic if you've just met. It's tyrannical, though the origin of the notion to do so may be totally understandable.

Being what you describe as "mentally ready to commit" is the easy part. That's merely intellectual. As a former ski racer, you can see the course, you know the line, etc. That's the easy part. Committing yourself to that is the other part, and how able anybody is able to run that course is in nobody's control. The secret of course is to let go. The only way to get anywhere is to let go of these and other controls; that is, as you describe yourself, what being "open-minded and easygoing" are.

Egbert

Hi, not2spookie,

I know you said not to bother you if I were the kind of person who took himself too seriously, but I really like that shiny gray scarf you're wearing and couldn't resist taking a poke at *Life of Pi* which is one of my least favorite books ever read, though not my "latest." To me, that book was a total bathetic ploy of jerk-off sentimentalism earmarked to make a big buck. See? I take myself too seriously. Or, maybe that isn't what you mean at all by it. I mean, sure, I like to laugh. Even Karl Rove likes to laugh. No, Karl Rove likes to laugh probably a lot more than most people. Of course he laughs at the wrong things because he's Karl Rove. There I go again: taking myself too seriously. I saw the Dalai Lama a couple of years back. He looked out beyond the fence, over the graveyard on his right, stretched out his arm, pointed there, and, before he began his talk to the crowd of people seated near him in the grass of a local baseball outfield, smiled, and then said, "The final destination!" I take myself about that seriously. How about you?

Egbert

Hi, Snow38,

You sound like fun. Of course I'm fun and all those things you say you want. So many women's profiles break it down to either labeling guys as lowlife game players or future husbands of their two future children, they tend to overlook that it is essential to "have a blast and enjoy life in our moment," as you put it. And me, I just don't fit into either of those two slots. Read my profile over, and if you think it's worth trading some emails back and forth, let's give it a shot.

Egbert

Dear Asiangrl75:

There's nothing wrong at all with your still being single. No one would ever think twice about a guy being single at any age, why a woman? As for your comment about guys just wanting to "play, play, play"; first off, we're guys. We like to play. Guys who don't like to play anymore, they're basically dead to me; they're just suits, lifeless and dry-cleaned. You, however, look and sound like a lot more fun than that. Get what you deserve, is my feeling on it. But, you've got some additional troubles, many of which probably have to do with your being perceived as being an Asian girl, and the host of American-based stereotypes that that involves or evokes in many men. Obviously, you don't fit that, aren't that: you're confident, able, independent, in charge, etc. So, some guy's going to have to see past all the external, which, is the first thing one gets with you: Wow, check out that hot, tall Asian chick! So, your email communication-first idea vs. just another pick-up at the bar is smart. I already see WHAT you are; now there's a chance to get WHO you are, and the same goes for you.

Egbert

Hi, Roseyfuture222:

No offense, but I don't believe a word of your profile.

Nobody who looks as beautiful as you do picture after picture after picture needs Match or anybody to find her way out of anywhere; I don't care if it's Detroit, Lima, or Shanghai, as the case may be. And if you are for real, that might be worse. Any man who was in your company would give up his entire life just to look at you for a straight hour. I thank the dog of Egypt that if in fact you are indeed for real, if the writing is yours, which is perfect by the way, and goes along with the person represented in the photos, by the Great Pyramid's cornerstone, I thank great Isis herself, nay, I thank Osiris, I thank the hands that tore the poet himself to pieces and threw his remains in the river, that you are thousands and thousands and thousands of miles away.

Egbert

Dear Everlucky,

You're right; a simple "hello" can lead to unexpected and good places. Few people, even here, are, I have found, willing to go even that far — just a "hello." I'm not sure why. Of course I think most people on Match would like to stumble or bump into someone they end up loving, but these same people, I think, exclude the possibilities of meeting people who could just as well end up as good friends. Without a "hello," nothing at all is possible — neither a friendship you speak of, nor a love you hope for. Your profile and your perspective leave genuine and good possibilities open, and create, I feel, a good chance for you to meet and know different people, and maybe with the "coincidence" of my looking at your profile once, and then your looking at mine once, the chance that that creates for you and I to know each other. It could turn out to be called very good luck, indeed, which is what we all do hope for, for ourselves, and, in the best of worlds, all others, too.

Egbert

Dear Firehouse5:

I regret I rested on my hooves too long. From time to time, I trotted out to the edge of the forest, caught a glimpse of you, and trotted back within the safety of elves, dwarves, and other sprites who knew me well. You were magnificent. Every so often, I would gallop to the perimeter; often you were there. Yes, there were others; I bowed to them, they patted my horn. I even whinnied, as a unicorn does, you know, from time to time, but ran away. I could not forget you. In the middle of a bower, tucked deeply within the oldest trunks of all, I folded my legs in thought, and brought you to mind. I was determined this time to leave the safety of my forested world and greet you. I did; you spoke to me; you said to me, "Indeed, you are a silly thing!" With that, you won my heart. I bent at my knees to carry you thither, wherever that should be. But, alas, you told me, too, that you had spied another. I shambled back into my reckless paradise, hearing the distant thunder breaking faraway.

Egbert

Dear Moviemiss,

Every guy who's writing you about maybe having a baby is a liar or not worth your intelligence. I mean look at all the things you do. You are amazing, a walking weapons of mass destruction! You're playful, and weird, and classy, and comfy, and, creative, and syntactical, and rebellious, and altogether radical. No, no, no, you need — if you do need an XY at all, which I doubt — someone who looks rather elegant, definitely handsome, well-mannered, *qui parle francais assez bien*, and who is (within in it all) a brilliant artistic creative madman — not a male wet nurse or some handy-andy milksop. By the way, I'm not the milksop nor the wet nurse.

yrs.,

Egbert

Dude, aka AMd511:

Not only did you "grow up like a tomboy," you write like a guy. Only guys write like, "I did this. I did that," (unless you're one of those "Russian ladies" who is trying to scam some desperate middle-aged loser who thinks he's special because a table of four con artists thousands of miles away in West Africa have got the love-squeeze on his money). Don't get me wrong; it's not that I don't like it. I think like a girl does most of the time. A little bit of this. A little bit of that. Give me a subject; give me a predicate — I know what to do with them, but I wonder what it would be like to date them? Let me tell you a lie I love telling (because of your confession of loving music but not being able to carry a tune): I've looked a hundred people in the eye and told them I've got perfect pitch like it was about as interesting to me as red and blue mixed make purple. Perfect pitch? My foot! Does that qualify as having a warped sense of humor? Even if we never meet, or if we do and don't turn out to be each other's "kindred spirit," you look and sound like a terrific person.

Egbert

Dear Editor:

Your eyes look blue in your primary shot. And I am the best living writer in the United States. Most are not. Did I care about Updike's death? As a man, may he rest in peace. As writer, one of the worst. I read all his shit when I lived in Budapest, before it was turned into Boston. There was a tiny foreign bookstore, a shelf of English writers. I had read little Updike before that, and wanted to be able to back up my feelings of dislike with authority. 2,000 pages later of Rabbit shit, I came to that conclusion. Does this qualify me in any way? Your eyes look blue. It's the framing of your face, your smile. Your bone structure would suggest "blue." Once a month, in 1985, I had to report to the rendorság, the Hungarian police. My visa, after I was interviewed in Hungarian by a cross female police official, was stamped again. "You are a writer?" she had said initially in English. "We don't like when you say bad things about us." Could Updike write about this? I wish he had. Not the flat, metaphor-dead, heart-dead, life-dead prose he wrote. I was hit by cops for bad things I did. I made love with a woman once in the dirt in the park at night and jumped up and yelled "*Disznó!*" at the eyes I caught behind her that were no more than a foot away from the bushes watching us. Your blue eyes will read this again someday. I will give you a copy of it. It's fiction now, but it won't be anymore. It's a lot better than that jackass Rabbit. It's just what I do, the little piece of godhead in me. Most don't. I have the little piece of rabbit shit still left in me. With your blue eyes, I might have had more luck.

Egbert

Hi, Cometochina,

Whether it's intentional or not, there's a stunning contrast between the pictures you've posted of yourself as an agent of harmony, simplicity, and beauty; and those of the world (and even the universe) as an agent of discord, fractals, and chaos. Sometimes this is evident in a single frame, as in, for instance, the picture of scattered brown leaves with your human shadow (as complete form) essentially burned into it. As though to hide your weariness of seeing itself, you cover your eyes in the darkness with sunglasses in some pictures (and expose only your own complete, human beauty); while in others, you reveal your very weariness with your sunglasses off as if to show that you have succumbed yourself to the lined and folded and cracked world around you. But this world, at the same time, as with the demolition picture of the building, has a particular beauty of its own — a sort of vinelike destructive beauty, an aesthetic of which you, too, are included and which you fully accept by revealing yourself in it. The lasting permanence of this aesthetic is captured as though destroyed forever, too, in the winter picture of the snow-blocked dam, or perhaps it is a canoe straddling that frozen stream that is seemingly thwarted by it.

Really great stuff.

Egbert

Xo ("Cometochina")

Xo had just moved from Wisconsin to Chappaqua. She struck me, from what she said, as sudden and impulsive. Except for a rack of teeth that stuck out of her mouth, a feature that was obscured by the two-dimensional nature of her pictures online, she was a knockout. Here she was in the middle of the country's worst financial disaster since 1929, having kicked off a cellulite-reducing company totally on her own in a little studio office near the banks of the Hudson River in one of the more affluent suburbs of the Northeast.

I have to say, though, that Xo, who never told me how to correctly pronounce her name, acknowledging only that it was too difficult, barely made time for me. We met in her office suite itself. I sat, actually, like a prospective client, and she like herself at work at her desk. The arrangement to go out for coffee didn't happen.

A good deal of my talk focused on her high school-aged son. She was totally clueless, apparently, about his switching school systems in the middle of the year and coordinating his records for his applications to college. As a reasonably well-educated person, it was an easy subject for me to discuss, and I felt comfortable offering any advice, if she needed any. She was sharp enough, clearly in her own right intelligent and motivated, to get the whole school situation, but also seemed optimistically blind to what I saw as the possibility of her son's just slipping through the system's cracks; mostly, it seemed because she was unaware of the importance or even the existence of timelines, test dates, and application deadlines — all the while believing her son was going to college in the fall.

I thought we were having a delightful time, even if the conversation seemed to get more and more out of control with anecdotes and laughter and excitement. It was only a moment after I had had the fantasy of having sex with her behind the sheet she had hanging from the ceiling to the floor to create a private space for clients she was treating, and had thought about the lovely clicking sound of the bolt fitting into the receptive notch when she turned the handle of the front door's lock, that she started frantically trying to reach her son, who was supposedly asleep still at home, by phone. There may be no connection between my moment's natural prurience and my ogling a pleasing bulge to her upper midriff out of desire however briefly when she stood up, and her frantically having the need to find her teenaged son. In any case, she broke off our meeting and, once outside her suite, before she drove off, I had to practically shove my hand into hers to shake it goodbye.

CHAPTER ELEVEN: JACKIE ("Gemstone_10021")

LETTERS:

Dear Happylife

Dear Lilac09

Dear Princess9026

Dear Designer07

Dear Flk6041

Hi, Pattiwumprat

Dear Desirewithfaith

Dear Blinky009

Dear Breckgirl68

Dear Sunflower212

Dear Gemstone_10021 [1]

Dear Jackie (Gemstone_10021) [2]

C'mon, Jackie (Gemstone_10021) [3]

Chere Jackie (Gemstone_10021) [4]

STORY: Jackie ("Gemstone_10021")

Dear Happylife,

You are definitely full of yourself, and that's good. Your entire profile reeks of self-possession, arrogance, and most of all desire. Frankly, I can't stand all the tepid screwing around on this site. Nice ladies wanting nice guys. I don't even fake trying to be one of those. I am so far off the charts, nobody practically dares to write me back. Those who do, they're the cream of the crop. Every one has been smart, bold, and educated. Rules? My rules work like this. If I like you, I will get in my car and drive to see you. Or, you will get on the train and come to see me. I am not interested in playing pat-a-cake with you or anybody else I see. I, too, have no intention of "rushing into anything serious right now." That does not mean I am hunting either for a mere sex partner. I have turned that down enough. I certainly won't change my persona to "get" you, and will not want you if you change yours to "get" me. Both of these are turnoffs to me. I am out here for making a connection, a real one. I will know that by how you look when I see you, how we meet for the first time, how you smell up close, and what you say. And if it all adds up, there will be great passion between you and me. That is what I am aiming for.

Egbert

Dear Lilac09:

Pardon me for saying so, but it sounds like your ideal is the stereotypical WBM (White Boring Man). You know, some guy who smiles broadly, but doesn't smirk (doesn't even know how to); a guy who genuinely drinks two Scotches on the rocks, but has never been stupid on bourbon; a man who believes traveling means to have a 12-day itinerary of European capitals and hotels tucked inside his lapel pocket (and has never in his life even once thought of hitchhiking in Vermont); a man who regards lovemaking as desirable (but only in the dark on weekends). Yuck.

Pardon me for saying so, but you do not seem to be this type at all! You seem beautiful and fiery and full of life. You sound like you are full of dimension and wonder and doubt. You sound like you genuinely love adventure and discovering the unknown, both the interior of your soul, and the untold secrets of the great world itself.

Do you really just want a man to hold the car keys, to know where you're going, to steady you when you're tipsy, to remind you of your pill when you forget, to keep your calendar, mind the books, open the champagne with a deft movement, and give your children his surname like Whitman or Greer or Entwistle? Pardon me for saying so, but why tie yourself down, why limit yourself to such a boring old stick?

Pardon my saying so, but I think you deserve a helluva lot more and a helluva lot better than that.

Egbert

Dear Princess9026:
You are fearless;
so am I.
I am fun;
so are you.

I am stubborn.
You look great.
So do I.
You are stubborn.
I like that.
Look me over.
If you like it,
ask me some questions
you'd like to ask.
I'll answer.
I myself don't ask
questions much.
You'll tell me what
you want to.
If this works, then
we can plan the next
step. Sound good?
I am fearless;
so are you.

You are fun;
so am I.

Egbert

Dear Designer07:

That's pretty funny your bit about "no pretension or game playing." You rattle off Sedona, Dubai, and Newport. How much more pretentious can you get? Oh, and I met Frank Gehry the other day. As for game playing, two of your pictures have you propped up against two different and gigantic beds whose one purpose is for some lucky gentleman to sleep in it with you, and the rest of your pix are of you with garments so sexually provocative Count Leo Tolstoy himself might give up his stance against the soul-numbing allure of amorous activity. I especially like that pic of you boob-touching the other chick. So, please, drop the façade: you present yourself as the hot, racy, globetrotting arm candy you definitely are. Be proud of it! Don't shield it under false pretexts of wanting some long-lasting picket fence and garden and a coupla cats in the window and an Easter lily given to you on Sunday by your balding husband. You are a fox who's way too hot for all that drek and middle-nothing success you and I know better as a middle class failure.

Egbert

Dear Flk6041,

The best thing about you, besides that décolleté shot of you that has earned you thousands of unwanted winks by dudes who have no prob closing down any shit-hole bar night after night playing the same dumbass game of pool with another loser, is your groupie story about selling falafels. Sounds like plenty of hummus and plenty of love. Don't get me wrong on this; I'm really not crass nor chasing young girls like you, but there is a certain freshness to your hopes, desires, and ambitions that I am happy to say makes a lot more sense to me than the usual nigh demands women closer in age to me are generally making. Once they get that special Upper East Side zip code, they're all business; they know how to flatter, but have lost the sweet ability to cajole. Don't let your love of New York and that degree you've got eat your spirit up. Keep with the falafel crowd; they're your bliss; they're your best.

yrs.,

Egbert

Hi, Pattiwumprat,

I have no use for people who aren't extreme. Extremes meet. Not my thought. It's Coleridge's. Unlike you, I'm not brief. The lists I keep are short. Perfection is boring. Good one. I like to be dazzled. Usually I have to be both the dazzler and the bedazzled. My puppet shows leave me hoarse and my fingers tired. I keep going back to your profile; I can't answer because I agree with so much of it. Or, I don't have to answer because what you say sounds so good.

You have no idea how good it feels to read the words, hear the mind of a smart woman.

I read a woman's profile on Match, swallow it, and mold my mind and answer to it. I can't do this to yours. It is because of this I feel, think, and believe I have something to learn from you. No puppet show. A conversation. Finally. Passion. Talk. Intelligence. I love these. Walking through a museum, nodding with our eyes. Agreeing with them. Pointing out things with a change in direction you're walking. Curious, you say? Yes. Endlessly. I think, I think, I'll begin with the Elephant's Child said the Crocodile, right? About the poor little crazy elephant with the snub nose who had Insatiable Curiosity? Some people just don't know when to stop. Some people can't. Some people just don't know what is good for them, right, too? Some people create and create. I create and create. Helen, tall ships, insomnia. Mandelstam. Writer: daytime insomniac. Blanchot. Writer, novelist, me.

Egbert

Dear Desirewithfaith,

Way back in December when I was just a newbie at this diabolical Matchgame, you know, the game where a guy takes his time to read a woman's profile carefully, drinks it in, and responds to it with care — that sort of rarity in your world of idiots, dumbass winkers, and grade-b jerk-offs hoping for a hoot — I got about nothing ever back. Was I too polite, too formal, too well-educated sounding and, God forbid, decent? Yes, alas, the curse of poor Hamlet and better breeding have always been upon me, plus a mind for dirtiness and passion, which, by the way you mention in your profile: Passion? I went skiing and practically broke my head off falling and being chucked in the woods last Saturday I was going so fast. "It doesn't get any better than that!" I said out loud to total strangers at the lodge when I told them about my mind-blinding wipe-out. That's passion. I come home from work, and get cranking on my fifth novel, or, more recently, the 58th short story that finished up the collection. This, I mail off to the publisher, when, happily, it was requested. How? Why? Passion. I write close to 300 hundred letters to beautiful, dazzling, intelligent, educated women on Match, all of whom seem to want a man with passion, a love of adventure, good conversation, and the desire to travel. Some write me back; most don't. Do I care? Somewhat, yes, definitely. I wish they ALL wrote me back. But they don't. And I go on because I always go on. Why? Passion.

Egbert

Dear Blinky009,

No disrespect intended, but the sexiest, nay, the most provocative profiles are from you Christian girls! Why is that? All the garbage that litters so many others' profiles — the dozen different countries they "love" to go to, the ridiculously high salaries that are supposed to be benchmarks of eligibility, the stacks of degrees from fancy schools — these are so blessedly not there in yours. Instead, there's just a beautiful you and God. Plain & Simple. Straightforward & True. You sound so good, too good to be true, that what you offer (unfortunately for me) strikes me as some sort of scam — the sort perpetrated by a table of four cigarette-smoking Russians working on some poor old hopeful middle-aged guy in America who really is just getting suckered into believed a young girl could possibly ever care for him — who believes it all enough to send her tons of money when she gets "stuck at customs" at the airport. These, at any rate are the stories I've heard that happen. But you don't seem to be that. What am I missing?

Egbert

Dear Breckgirl68,

Your profile made me laugh and want to weep. Your line about guys' profiles that are about sports-watching and their basically holding their own nuts to attract another man, that was fucking hilarious. Can I say "fucking" and not have it sounding like I, too, am really writing to a guy and tryin' to get to know 'im — unbeknownst to my professed heterosexual proclivities? Yes, I can. You are so on the money! Nevertheless, do you realize how much of your profile is devoted to shooing away these clowns? (and therefore displaces what you as a person have time and space to say about yourself). Wow, what a lady must have to put up with in this world! I mean, it sounds like all you've gotten in your life is hits by morons, catcalls by hardhats, and whippings by power ties. Somewhat timorously, may I make so bold as to ask if there's something fishy that you yourself are doing in dress, style, or affectation to bring it on — or is this just the way of the world for an attractive & intelligent woman who dares to show more than their eye slits in a world of testosterone-fueled, rose-crushing, thorn-biting dwarves, fools, and monsters?

Egbert

Dear Sunflower212:

Any fool can use chopsticks; it doesn't make him a nice guy.

Truly, I am a nice guy.

Truly, I am a dark horse.

Truly, I am a hyperborean wizard.

I am not one of those fools from the Midwest who cannot use chopsticks.

Egbert

Dear Gemstone_10021,

I guess I'm going to go first: there's something that intrigues each of us about the other, as shown by our scanning each other's profile a few different times on different occasions, but also something that has pushed both of us from away from contacting each other, too. However, I'm going to just stick with the pluses here. Probably, for me, it's your "passionate, romantic, and adventurous spirit" and stated optimism; these, combined with your drive to succeed, and the power that that requires, are all draws for me. And, too, as a father of a 19-year-old boy whom I absolutely love, and detect in you the same deep connection that you have with your own kids, all make you out to be quite a substantial person, even if that very phrase — "substantial person" — sounds a bit off or not quite what I mean. I, too, like you it seems, value being fit and active, and am at the gym several times a week; or, during the winter, off skiing at one of the local mountains close to where I live upstate. So, I've put my toes in the water, and you can see a little bit how I wiggle them; maybe you'll put yours in, too, now that I have, and show me how you wiggle yours.

Egbert

Dear Jackie (Gemstone_10021),

I sensed in your last email to me that you were getting "cold feet" about meeting me. I felt your questions were pretty much lined up to "crash the deal" but did my best to answer them.

They were, for instance, a far cry from your writing, as you had, "In terms of what I am passionate about...first and foremost, it's my children. Then it would be intelligent men! You do sound brilliant!:)" Here, you sound both hopeful and full of play. And while, sure, it's fairly plain that I'm brilliant, this is not, I think, the best reason to "fall" for me or not; rather, it would be my own life-playfulness (even though that hardly sounds so), and my willingness and ability to listen to another (which you could also call attentiveness), and my willingness & ability to feel the world around me (which you could also call sensitivity). "Brilliance" or "intelligence" is at the service or the behest of these, allowing me to articulate, to some degree, some of my so-called constituent parts, as David Hume might have it.

I really can't help playing, don't want to, and never will; this does not make me frivolous, insincere, or silly; rather, I think, quite the opposite. It means I am active and aware and full of the very breath of life itself. I am these; ample, fair, and strong (as Whitman put it about his grand matriarch America).

Honestly, Jackie, you asked me about what is "reasonable" (my mind flashed to a brilliant & playful section of Steven Pinker's book *How the Mind Works* in the index under "Romantic Love" — which I'm doing everything here I can besides pasting it for you, which I could, too, but think if it's really worth your time and curiosity you'll go to B & N and look it up yourself one day), and I can tell you upfront that there is nothing "reasonable" about it. Couched in terms of "dating" there is no point. With an eye turned toward, against, or around "marriage" (and her sometime sister "divorce"), may God be with us all.

But toward meeting someone you might fall for? Or whom I might fall for? These uncertainties, these blessings, I will never shirk from. It is, I suppose, a certain worldview, a definite *Weltanschauung* I have held and maintained at my very best — and, for that matter, forfeit at my worst; and then, to borrow a phrase from one of Joseph Conrad's doomed ship captains, I am like a man whose "head is wrapped in a wool blanket." However, I am much more the Lord Jim type: troublesome, rebellious, obstinate, passionate, and principled to the point of feeling, at least, but never performing, some murder in my bones (though not quite as tall as that eponymous hero.)

Know, though, for certain, I am not a murderer at all; it's only a convenient and immediate trope, which I don't feel like amending to play it safe. I don't play safe. Safe is unappealing to me, boring. Yes, I once knew a fine enough lady from the Upper West Side; it was so safe I thought my life was turning into being one of those mindless ant-bodies living inside a nibbled-away tunnel inside the plastic see-through case of one of Uncle Milton's Ant Farms for children. No, I like adventure: I drove down, just as I say in my profile essentially, at the drop of the hat, to buy a woman the finest bar of chocolate at Whole Foods recently. We had little in common; she never unbuttoned even her coat; I am happy I did so, and will be happy for it all my life. Reasonable? Absolutely not. Crazy? Absolutely not. Passionate, yes. Adventuresome, yes. Romantic, yes. Poetic? Absolutely.

yrs.,

Egbert

C'mon, Jackie (Gemstone_10021).

We're both gamblers. How about dinner 6:00, Saturday? If there's nothing there, there's nothing there. I just get out of there and beat it. And it'll still be early, early enough for you to enjoy the entire evening.

Egbert

Chere Jackie (Gemstone_10021),

Je t'ai ecrit peut-etre trois ou quatre fois deja maintenant,
mais tu ne reponds pas. Il faut dire que je suis etonne. J'ai
croye qu'il y avait quelque chose entre nous deux. Il faut
dire aussi que ton silence m'a blesse. Et pourquois "blesse"
tu pourais me dire? Imbecile, il n'y a pas aucune chose entre
"nous deux." Il y n'a pas ce que tu voudrais aimer appeler
— ou m'accuser — ici encore cette chose que tu t'appeles
quelque chose qui n'existe pas "nous deux." Enfin, monsieur, tu n'as pas aucune idee de moi! Tu ne me connais pas,
Egbert.

Tu as raison, madame. Parce que tu est une femme plus
capable de presque toute le monde, tu as raison, comme
d'habitude, Mademoiselle Jackie…Oui, on peut dire que tu
as raison parce que tu es vraiment plus capable de presque
tout le monde, comme j'ai dit deja.

Mais, au meme temps, il faut dire que tu m'as blesse, Jackie.
Enfin, je dois le dire.

Mais, comment?

Jackie, comme je t'ai dit avant, j'avais l'idee, j'avais l'es-
poir, que je m'ai trouve une femme intelligente, puissante,
et belle. Les trois m'ont bouge. Je te voulais connaitre. Tres
simple. Au meme temps, tu m'as dit plusieurs fois quelque
choses complementaires. Et naturallement, j'aime ca. Apres
nous nous avons ecrive deux ou trois semaines, tu m'as
plaisais encore plus. Naturallement, n'est ce pas? Ah, je me
suppose que j'aimais le frommage que tu as laisse tombe
dans ma bouche. Mais il faut dire aussi que je ne resemble
pas cette fable ecrit de Racine pour les enfants, ni le pau-
vre Monsieur Corbeau. Je n'ai pas une plumage si laide, ni
un esprit si rude, ni une ame remplit avec les paroles vains.
Pardonnez-moi, mais pas moi, madame. Au contraire, je me
semble un oiseau presque royale, pas exactement le fils d'un

diplomate, mais assez bien eleve. Ca va dire seulement que je sais comment je dois me debrouiller, comment je devrais me conduire dans la vie avec l'honneur, et l'integrite, avec le coeur humain et la bonhomie toujours avec tout le monde; quelque chose Monsieur Thomas Jefferson de mon pays s'a appele "l'aristocratie naturalle," moi un paysan juif perdu, un pequenaud chretien trouve, un enfant du paysage russe et des montagnes americains, une athee de dieu partout, un homme du monde ici.

Fache. Blesse. Desole.

Il y a vingt-six ans que j'ecris de la langue francais, mais j'espere que tu peux me comprendre.

Egbert

Jackie ("Gemstone_10021")

I had some of my highest hopes for Jackie P. From our Match emails, prior to our actually meeting, I could tell she was powerful, intelligent, well-educated, accomplished, and classy. She was beautiful and she was independent, and I like these things. I have to confess, too, I was a bit of a sucker for her calling me brilliant and complimenting me on my writing — samples of which were just my notes to her. Even before we had met, she brought out much of my charm and desire, my desire to connect with someone on an equal level, in a certainly kind and possibly loving way. I felt that Jackie and I had the chance, in the best way, to be on par with each other.

I also have to say, though, that I had to reach pretty deeply into both my inner resources, which are of the heart, and into my abilities, which are of the mind, to bring off our chance to connect with each other. She was no easy person to win over, to impress. She was no pushover. Unlike me, who is fairly impetuous and definitely impulsive — I'm the type of guy who sees when the wind is up that it'd be a perfect day to fly a kite and will go far out his way then to find a store that sells kites to fly one, who'll interrupt his own narrative to make up another, so blown away am I by my own passions — Jackie could express definite interest while at the same time exercise realistic caution. This much I could extract from her brief self-effacing emails back to me that got to the point and expressed little more than the point itself, typical of persons of her caliber and profession as an entrepreneurial dealmaker. I had a friend once whose brilliance at making money was his ability to kernelize huge amounts information which then allowed him to see a whole situation clearly and act upon it swiftly. Jackie had this, too.

Still, the history remains that when Jackie emailed me on her Blackberry from Costa Rica on a business trip, it made me feel good. It made me feel important. It made me feel that what I was saying was important to her. And who doesn't like to feel special? I felt she was special, and she had shown me signs that she felt the same way about me, too.

However, for reasons I will never know, she quite out of the blue stopped contacting me. This followed a number of questions she had posed and which I had answered. Geographical questions, such as her pondering the wisdom of her dating a man who lived almost two hours away from her, to which I replied with élan that traveling to see her would not be a problem for me. Marital questions, such as wanting to know when exactly I had been divorced, to which I replied my marriage had fallen apart half a year prior. And the like. She suddenly became stalwart in her unresponsiveness. As I was moving forward, she was retreating. Or, I should say, she had altogether retreated.

Most men, I suppose, would have stopped there, would have read the writing on the wall, and called it a day with her. Men are generally as dumb as sperm. They batter away willy-nilly like whales that will just as gladly live in the ocean as they will just as freely beach themselves and die. But something in me is not like most men. Paint me the romance artist who loves, who feels ardor, who feels like Hamlet but is, I must also confess, as dangerous sometimes as Raskolnikov (not to imply that Hamlet isn't dangerous, but he's dangerous of another kind). This sort of man is a different sort of man altogether. He will go to all ends, he will sail the earth, he will span the globe, he will never ever give up on the object of his love until all mercies are exhausted. And I, for better or for worse, am like this.

And so, I continued to pursue Jackie. It was, finally, when I wrote Jackie a letter length email entirely in French — which, as a daughter of a diplomat, she had listed in her online profile as one of the several languages she knew, and was more French than I have written in my entire life since college papers on Camus, and which, too, required that I get out my Bescherelle from high school to double check some of my past participles — that she wrote me back that she was impressed with my persistence and proposed she should at least meet me for a drink.

I was overjoyed.

To her changing of the time to meet from late Saturday afternoon to twelve so that she could play golf at 2:00, I was amenable. I understand of course that she had placed a boundary, a curtain on our engagement. No matter what, it would be natural for us to depart from each other regardless of how well or how poorly our initial engagement went. To Jackie's showing up just close to half an hour late at the posh & crowded City Limits diner in White Plains, as she had suggested, which was otherwise in the middle of nowhere for me, whose parking lot was filled with BMW's, Mercedes, and Lexuses, I was also amenable. She was every bit as classy, poised, and beautiful as I had imagined and hoped. She was stable, articulate, and deeply intelligent. Moreover, and this was the most striking, she was absolutely comfortable; she was so comfortable in her own skin, that it nigh knocked me out of mine. I, as I lurched toward her in an unseemly manner, like a guerrilla fighter betraying State secrets in the reeds to an informer, was everything I was not. My own poise, confidence, and mien of self-possession were shot to hell.

Primarily, this had to do with two sides of my nature at war, I think, with each other — one of which is delightful, loving, and caring; and the other which is plotting, calculating, and prepared to prosecute. There I was, seated in front of a beautiful and fit woman who is the principal of her own financial firm, a graduate of Duke University, the Wharton School, a mother of two children, an alumna of Hotchkiss

— a well-born child, successful daughter, woman of distinction; there I was, seated in a booth before a dream-powerful person who is straightforward, clear, and honest, who has been duly impressed, too, with me. And here I am, too, with a briefcase at my side with reams of information on Jackie from sleuthing out small details in her emails, cross-referencing these with those in her profile, and foremost from the breach of security she had allowed from my following up on the careless electronic signature she'd — against the Match protocol of anonymity to turn such preferences on such devices off — inadvertently left behind when she had emailed me from Costa Rica wherein she had supplied me with her all-important surname. It was really due to the latter that the whole panoply of Jackie P. was opened up to me and I was able to, along with the redundancy of her having used the same photograph of herself in several online places, corroborate everything. I had her educational record; I had her employment history; I had read her associates' commendations and could chime lines from these, making her think my words were the kindnesses of similar happenstance when they echoed in the tunnels of her dulled remembrances past, while I watched her smiling somewhere to herself on the inside there. I knew the average value of homes in her neighborhood. I knew the ethnic and age breakdowns of her block. I could project her income. I knew the online clubs she belonged to. I had residences (past and prior), zip codes (past and prior), area code (same). I had a Google snapshot of her house on the corner of her street where she lived in Mamaroneck. I could see her garage. Most of all, I knew her birthday. I had her real age, forty-seven, a Virgo born on September 7, not forty as she claimed her age was beneath the thumbnail photo she had posted of herself in her on-line dating profile — the lie I could catch her in and parry, I thought to myself, the lie to my counter-lie that I had told her myself at the diner regarding my marital status as being divorced when the truth was I was currently separated. I could get her. When the time came, when the time was right. And, too, for the sake of fairness, so-called, to continue my inner-briefcased dialogue I had been having with myself for days before we actually met, I had done all the research and gathered all the available and pertinent information online one could possibly wish to know the background truths on me, to gallantly save her the trouble of having to do so herself. These included my father's scientific accomplishments, the vast medical accomplishments my grandfather had made, my own awards and accomplishments; and, to complete the gesture of sweeping honesty, my wedding announcement in the *New York Times*. Awful, really. And all of this information which I had acquired with the steadfast use of the internet, plus $2.95 for the services of Intelius, not to mention hijacking my wife's LinkedIn account, I had printed up in hard copy and befittingly highlighted for Jackie's efficient reading. Secreted at my side I had all of these documents labeled and organized in black snap-back metal clips the whole while over 50 dollar poached eggs and hash browns, prepared at the right moment to unbuckle it all like an honest business deal, like an exchange of munitions for munitions, con for con, truth for truth. This, I had believed, quite foolishly, and madly even while I was driving to meeting Jackie for an hour-and-a-half that same morning, was how to seal the deal. This was how to do it. This I believed was how to make it with her. I was certainly out of my mind.

It would be fair, too, to say that Jackie did not give me much rope anyway. She had come late; and did, even though I joked with her about my always being on-call for my family, too, spend a heckuva lot of the time chatting on her cellphone with her sister, and eating up more time — our time — when she ducked away to the restroom, returning to our table with the device still pressed to the side of her head. Honestly, behavior like that is just plain rude.

I have to say that even though she treated me a little bit like a burr that got stuck on the side of her sock, I had a thing for her. I did, though in many ways I did shoot myself in the foot many times when I had brunch with Jackie P., feel bad about the whole thing. I really did have a crush on this very impressive woman. Sure, I know, she treated me like shit a little bit, barely penciling me in for little more than an hour of her time to be taken out by a gentleman for an expensive freebie before teeing off, I am aware of this; but I still liked her. Even when I shook her hand and said goodbye and kissed her on the cheek and knew it was forever, I still did.

CHAPTER TWELVE: ELOISE ("ELOISE12222")

LETTERS:

Dear SometimesBelieve

Dear Bettynyc90

Dear Lovestruck3443

Dear Dqcws

Dear Fifipine

Dear Nycchinyc

Dear Vittovoo

Dear Vapo241

Hi, Tulipsantana

Hi Mindy54321

Hey, Geewhiz

DEAR ELOISE12222

STORY: Eloise ("ELOISE12222")

Dear SometimesBelieve:

As an entrepreneur, you know that, like business, Match is a game, and, too, like business, a very serious one. That said, it is not clear, however, what its rules are. Beyond obvious indecency and cruelty, there is little to regulate any of its activities. There is no prescribed code of commitment, and, therefore, nothing to intercede should there be the breach of the latter.

Thus, as you state that you are "NOT into games, and [are] actually quite tired of them," I feel obliged to point out to you that, while at the top of your profile you indicate that you are "not sure" about having children, you later declare quite emphatically not to contact you unless you wish to have them. This contradiction, I would hazard to say, is a breach of the game of internal consistency. In your picture, with your chin poised thoughtfully and your pearls draped natu- rally, and your beautiful and penetrating face gazing straight through the mind of one more man dull and uxorious, you certainly look like quite an elegant and sophisticated and al- together intelligent catch; the reader, roped in by something rather uncommon on Match, then is led into your quan- dary of birth and children. Naturally, this is your right, and I hope you achieve what you wish for, but, I must note that, as a fellow Virgo, one who admires analysis & discrimina- tion as much as he admires taste & class, which you have, as I have intimated, in more than ample amounts, you are not playing a straight game of pool here; and, I think, it might be working against your stated better purpose.

Egbert

Dear Bettynyc90,

Honestly, madam, I would not know where to begin even to define what salient characteristics begin to define the so-called nonconventional man. Does he pick his teeth at dinner? Does he actually look at Seurat from the proper focal length, not like the tourists breathing all over the colors? Does he think Plato funny? Does he dig Radiohead? Does he use the word "dig" in italics and remember *The Warriors* and the tail end of the sixties bled through into the 70's? Does he wear a red velvet jacket to work, or a blue one of the same material? Does he drive into Manhattan just to buy an ugly girl a bar of the world's best chocolate? Does he speak his mind, even when it is likely to be offensive? Is he a constant performer? Will he break your balls and soothe your headaches? Will he make you chicken soup when you're sick and drive the pot of it to Boston? Will he fly across the Atlantic with a hardbound copy of Keats to give to you? Will he give 20 bucks to a crack whore and talk with her for an hour while she smokes it up? Will he watch Spencer Tracey whack Katharine Hepburn's butt ten times in a row just to see her smile her love smile? Will he offhandedly tell off people he doesn't know that there is no recession so long as he sees them queued up buying rosemary shrimp at $19.99/lb? Will he cancel his Facebook three weeks after opening it because he doesn't want all that contact? Will he for years pedal on the elliptical machine with his eyes closed the whole time, listening to Glenn Gould and Nirvana? Will he befriend and mourn the janitor who just died last week, and hate most of his colleagues? Will he win awards and try to seduce any one of three sisters? Will he buy flowers for all the receptionists because they were kind? Will he forbid even his own son to read certain works of his? Ever. Will he almost weep seeing three Van Goghs tucked in the corner yesterday at MoMA? Will he clean his house naked? Will he continue twenty-three years after the fact to dream of his dead friend dying in the dream in his arms, again and again, and wake up both joyful for this visitation and distraught over this loss?

You tell me, but I don't pick my teeth at the table.

Egbert

Dear Lovestruck3443,

Don't get me wrong, but I'd hate to be you. You must get 200 hits a day, and every hit is a lie. Maybe one or two aren't. But with such an overwhelming flood of men who are just gaga about thinking they have even a chance in hell of a snowball not melting to sleep with you, which is the only thing 198 of them can see for a snowflake; not more than one, maybe two have even seen winter, can no less spell it, can no less write a half-intelligent email, if even to imagine inside their dumbass heads one clear sentence. But, you know, that's just guys!

But, honey, who can blame these idiots? You do the wind up to reveal some of your tragic character flaws, which might make twenty of these lunkheads not email you, and the worst thing you confess to is that you spend too much money on coffee! And as for sleeping in late, do you think Paris wanted his stolen Helen to go feed the chickens bright and early in the morning. Hell, no! Not one heterosexual guy in 3 billion, unless you discount farmers, is going to kick you out of his bed before 10 o'clock A.M., if he can help it.

Now, you wanted a best friend? Well, I am giving you a best friend's advice. There is nothing in your profile that works to screen all these dopes! That pic of you with the bare midriff, whoah! Look at my profile, for instance. It looks so snobby and elitist and intimidating and Mr. Spiritual-I-Am-Buddha-Genius-Man that almost nobody writes me! Am I really like this? Of course not! Am I lying? No, but I am SCREENING so that I can actually pick with a clear head and clean fingers. It's like picking out fruit at the store, or avocados: you turn a few over, squeeze them a little bit at the ends — but who'd be able to pick anything if you had to go through a million avocados before you could choose? You couldn't. Well, that's just my advice; you don't have to take it; I won't feel bad.

I am very curious to know how it's going for you? I'm sure that a woman as beautiful as you are has a lot to say about the guys basically drooling over their emails to you over this whole matter.

Egbert

Dear Dqcws:

Your profile cracks me up. You don't want "serial daters" yet, besides the fact that you've been roaming these e-pages for years now yourself, fail to apparently get that this forum is made for junkies. Who the hell doesn't have tea with someone and, shortly upon returning home, check to see who else has landed on the tarmac? And, of course, since all of us here in our forties, unless there's something deeply and probably irrevocably wrong with us because we have not been married or significantly attached to another thus far in our lives, all of us have some sort of attachment issues made manifestly clear by virtue of the fact that we are no longer married or significantly attached. Obviously, it's more complicated than that, but we are all, after all, quite responsible for whom we chose in the past to be our partners — and chose persons with whom such lifelong attachment failed; because, well, we probably had these "attachment issues" playing themselves out somewhere, somehow. And, as I said, it is obviously more complicated than that rather facile explanation. But I still find it sad and somehow amusing that you feel the urge, nay, the necessity of spelling out that you don't want a guy who's still pissed off over: a) losing; b) feeling/being fucked over by his ex; or, even worse, in love with her. Wow, what kind of drek have you attracted, Doctor? Or, is this the general inpatient Match diagnosis? Still, your own attachment issues, like wolves, are howling in the night loud and clear: smack up in your profile you assert the need and requirement for a man, at this point completely anonymous, to "promise" you something. Isn't that sort of demand, which it is, a little premature? I think so. It also points to a deeper and more significant issue of your own questions over your own self-worth; people who are sure of themselves do not, especially even before the first blush, make others make promises to them. Doing so is totally suffocating, stifling. The only promise you can expect is, after a volley of emails, a guy you're interested in shows up at the right place on time to meet you. That's it. And that, by the way, is actually quite a significant step, going as it is from the disembodied and incorporeal to the embodied and corporeal. It's really huge. Self-confidence, self-worth, self-belief begin at the point where you feel that, just as you are, people themselves will feel, unto and for themselves, to chuck in a little Kant (strangely) here, the desire to promise themselves to you. Why? Because you are you! They see that and want to be with you — which, after all, is what all of us want, desire, and deserve: to be seen and heard, just as we are — in all our human glory and shortcomings. Small pointers: you, especially given your education and job, really ought to clean up the errors that mar your profile: "charecters" is a misspelling, and you mean "complement," as in the sort that makes two things together complete, not the "compliment" one as in, "Hey, I really like that belly button ring of yours."

Egbert

Dear Fifipine:

You're not giving much here except a little skin, a little sun-tan line, and a little hip-lilt. It's all very seductive, in a proper sort of way of course; and, I suspect, you are very much the same: both proper and seductive. Write back; give a guy little more!

Egbert

Dear Nycchinyc,

You are the first woman I've clicked on that I wanted to say, "God, what a beauty!"

You sound incredibly smart and even though you live next to that nasty town Greenwich where I grew up, definitely are a mind worth knowing.

Egbert

Dear Vittovoo,

If you like Levin, you'll like me. If you like the scene when he's drinking *kvas* with the *muzhiks* best of all moments in all literature best, then you'll like me. If you like the fact that in my twenties, I slept in a little grotto tucked away in Stockholm where an assassin had once hidden, then you'll like me. If you like the fact that I once wrote a letter to a boy I was jealous over in the exact same style as the illiterate letter in *Lucky Jim* goes, then you'll like me. I know you like *Lucky Jim*; if that is the funniest book you've ever read, then you'll like me. And I mean made you laugh out loud hard. Real hard. And the next time you read it, years later, too. If you like that I have written five novels, then you'll like me. If that is more important than the fact that none is published yet, then you'll like me. If you like the fact that a book length collection of short stories is sitting on the desk at Dalkey Press right now, then you'll like me. If you like the fact that I tell you that these short stories, are god-awful brilliant (and I do mean "god-awful"), then you'll like me. If you think that this *if p, then q* logic is sorta funny, then you'll like me.

Egbert

Dear Vapo241,

Your profile is a quick kick in the pants funny and smart, just the way I like it. And you sound like one of the few who hasn't aborted her mind for what at best could be called compensation, and at worst a waste of one's brains over living her life tucked under an ever larger and larger financial security blanket. No, as you write, you anticipate what your reader might think as the syllables are just beginning to crawl their way up his throat. That is part of what makes you, to my eye, playful and fun. So few are. Really. Now, since I saw your profile last night, I've been pondering telling you about this, and I'm still doubting myself. Ne'ertheless, as Hector says to his eager battle bound brethren when he turns on his heel and decides, against his better judgment to wage war against the Greeks on behalf of his lazy brother for Helen, your rather cryptic line about "cuddling in black cabs," and even more, your vow to "never, ever make [me] wait outside the dressing rooms at Ann Taylor" prompts me to go on. The last time I was at Ann Taylor, and accompanied a woman into one of the changing rooms with a heap of dresses, afterward the manager came over to me and told me I was not permitted to be where I had been and politely escorted me out of the general changing area. With a healthy and cheerful glow adding good color to my face, I simply replied, both measured and polite, that I was helping zip up the back of said lady's dress, which, in a manner of speaking, I had, too. "Yes," she said, "but you're not allowed in there." It is at such moments as these that one's so-called breeding, education, and poise come to the fore, and are at one's most delicious & exquisite service. "Cheeky" enough for ya?

Egbert

Hi, Tulipsantana,

Thanks for the wink. Your writing is awesome and your points are right on. You and I both sound like we know how important play is. From that, everything else blooms, everything else is created.

There is, as I'm sure you know, too, a huge, huge difference in being childish, which is just being immature and irresponsible, and childlike. You sound like the sort of person who has held onto her vital being childlike, which is where wonder and curiosity come from. Like you, too, I work hard during the day, but remain alive long into the night. It's a nice picture you paint of yourself cooking in the kitchen "something tasty" — not as a duty, but as an enjoyment, a pleasure, one that's also coupled with a sense of joy-filled generosity to others. I also like the distinction you make between being confident and being narcissistic. Confident people, I think, have a bowl full of a healthy sense of being in the world — and they can give plenty away. Narcissists, I think, believe their bowl is full, but it's really pretty empty: they have little or nothing to give anyone; they're essentially starving people, who believe, falsely, that they have something, even lots, to give away. Often, the two, at first, can resemble the other; and, too, the one can be mistaken for the other. Did I get a little over-analytical here? Yup. Me, it's just my way of trying to say "thank you" to you and to connect. I hope to hear back from you.

Egbert

Hi Mindy54321,

You ask, "Who will marry me?" Just from the joyfulness captured in your picture, I'd think you'd get 50 marriage proposals a day! Only a very, very special man will ever deserve to marry you, for there is a quiet radiance in your words that promises to reveal a bursting glow of life & energy. And, too, I can sense there is a deep underlying complexity to you as well, a good kind of complexity. Who else would keep in the same household cats & birds!

While I'm not going to change it anytime soon, I'm afraid that my own profile is a lot drier than I am. I'm not, not by a long shot. I'm playful, and fun, and willing to go just about anywhere with someone who, even if you're "quiet at first" whispers to me where she'd like.

Egbert

Hey, Geewhiz,

You're just the kind of trouble I like. Behind your sado-masochistic array of words, I know you're just a romantic angel falling headlong first into the lap of love. You can't feel or fool me for a second. But, you're really wrong about the dating bit. Are you kidding? This place is a paradise for successful daters. Even Stephen Fucking Hawking could make girls pine and yearn. And that, basically, is the lost art of romancing, isn't it? Some dude with the right amount of DNA to thrill your shot glass with, who's witty and smart enough to make that little rictal smile of yours appear and wander off into the desert the same way that that poor great fool Enoch with God did. I am looking, prowling, a big Virginia Woolf-sized lighthouse on the lookout for an "adjective whore" just like you. Come on; come to Papa, and crash your vessel upon my rocks.

Egbert

DEAR ELOISE12222:

SINCE YOUR PROFILE IS IN CAPITAL LETTERS, I'M GOING TO WRITE YOU THE SAME WAY. I HAVE READ PLATO IN GREEK AND I CAN REPLACE A KITCHEN FAUCET. I CAN CHOP WOOD AND SKI FAST. I AM PASSIONATE, HIGHLY RESPECTED AT WORK; AND A PUBLISHED, BUT LESS WELL-KNOWN, WRITER.

ELOISE, IF THAT'S YOUR NAME, I BET YOU ARE BEATING OFF MEN LIKE FLIES ON A HOT SUMMER DAY BY NOW. WHY, BECAUSE YOU ARE THE ONLY ATTRACTIVE WOMAN ON THE INTERNET WITH BARE KNEES WHO IS NOT SAYING "MARRIAGE" IN ONE HAND, AND HOLDING A NOOSE IN THE OTHER.

MAYBE THIS DOESN'T SEEM LIKE IT, (MAYBE IT'S THE CAPITAL LETTERS MAKING ME BE THIS WAY), BUT I REALLY AM A "MATURE, INTELLIGENT, OUTGOING MAN." SERIOUSLY, YOU SOUND INTELLIGENT & FUN (A RARE AND WHOLLY DESIRABLE COMBINATION IN MY WORLD, AS YOU CAN SEE), BUT WATCH OUT: THERE ARE MILLIONS OF DOPES AND KNUCKLEHEADS OUT THERE. I COULD BE ONE MYSELF OF COURSE, BUT YOU CAN TELL, EXCEPT FOR THESE DAMN CAPITAL LETTERS THAT ARE DOING ME IN, THAT I'M NOT.

WRITE ME BACK! DO IT IN LITTLE LETTERS, PLEASE; AND LET'S SEE THE DIFFERENCE IT MAKES.

yrs.,

Egbert

Eloise ("ELOISE12222")

As soon as I met Eloise, I wanted to slip my arm around her waist. There was some magic in it. I didn't care a jot that her face was still beat up a bit with acne, even though she was 46. She was tall, or about 5'8", thin, and good energy came out of her. When we went to the ticket counter, where, since she was late and had called me already twice to let me know she'd be there in half an hour, I'd already bought mine, she paid for a MoMA membership and we quickly refunded the ticket I'd gotten to get another one for me for 5 bucks as Eloise's guest. It was light, breezy, and obvious what to do, and we did it with joy.

The money saved was a good break on an arugula and goat cheese salad I wanted to have at the museum bistro before we went to look at pictures, which, by the way, Eloise and I never did. Instead, we spent the entire time sitting side-by-side on stools at a long counter that faced the window. She shared some of my lunch with her own fork from my plate, and I had the feeling I could walk down the street with this woman for miles and miles with her pressed close to me. Maybe this was possible due to our understanding through an earlier email that I would be more like a gay friend to her than a boyfriend. But I think that our immediate sense of closeness was closeness some people just inexplicably have for each other.

Absolutely kind, she'd been bounced around a lot. She'd been married twice, the first time to a man she described as much older than she was and, too, who was her professor when she'd gone to Nova Scotia years back to go to college from China. The second time to some lawyer business shark who seemed to want to diddle other women as a side practice. For me, it was hard to hear about both — one seemed such an obvious Mr. White Fish & Chips takes advantage of the pretty young exotic thing story, and the other such a sleazeball arm candy affair, I couldn't look. But Eloise lacked any resentment or any bitterness over either. Rather, that she had become through it all independent and financially successful was obvious when she'd plopped down some platinum card to pay her museum dues at the beginning of our date. She'd ridden the real estate wave selling luxury condos when the market crested and had made close to a million dollars. She was so successful, she now helped her first ex-husband, with whom she had a teenage daughter, pay his rent. And as for the second, she'd signed away all legal rights to any of this man's considerable assets because he could not agree to give her anything, she told me, "from his heart."

If it's not too unfair to type people, I'd met the likes of Eloise before. I had a girlfriend myself once like her. Good to the heart. And a little bit crazy. Women who ended up as cherished objects for men who really did not know how to cherish women — and so, in time, lost them. And while these women had a preternatural goodness about them that was almost too much, too true, to believe, whose strange visions of reality had nothing to do with either of them being anything but very intelligent, which they indeed were — it wasn't due to some inability to grasp and assemble the facts of reality — there was also, I must add, like a long ignored splinter that does not seem to have caused any real harm, or an injury that doesn't seem to have inflicted any lasting pain; there was, in the tail end of things, a lingering sense that some additional justice needed to be done by the men in their lives' pasts, to do for these women one final act of good. There was not, again, a sense of injustice that speaks of victimhood, but there was a real sense that in the interest of what was right in the world, men themselves needed to take one extra step. They needed to commit an act of grace. Eloise's first husband, while she described him as being the smartest person she'd ever met, she said point blank, looking down toward the plate glass window, that even though she had enjoyed lovemaking with him, he was "really not a man." She added with a mixture of shame and compassion for this man that he could not really support himself. She accepted this as one accepts a flaw in a piece of art, in the head of a Greek statue being knocked off. As for the second ex, who struck me as nearly villainous, she retained a hope for him that he would come about and give to her some of his financial largesse, long after the fact of their divorce, and this would show his own having come to a more complete understanding of himself. Which would be for his good. Cockamamie? Yes. Earnest? That, too.

I could see Eloise was wholly, or as close as one can come to it, without quite being a bodhisattva, without judgment. And this was over people in her life who had disappointed her, let her down, and betrayed her. Unlike me, who burned with anger and then was able, at my best, to forgive, it did not look as though Eloise went through this two-step process. She was like a castaway, dinged, beautiful bottle that washes up and is still beautiful, that washes up again, and is still beautiful.

"Men," she said, "propose to marry me all the time. A man just did on a second date. Sometimes on the first." I could see why. Eloise appealed to the goodness that is in all of us, even if we are not defined by it, even if we cannot live up to it. We want to. We want to love the Eloises of the world. She made men want to hold her and make love to her and walk proudly through the streets of Rome, Venice, and New York with her with their arms wrapped around her waist almost forever. She made me feel good. She made others feel good. She was a special person whose loss to me as a lover I felt for a good while after I learned for certain that she was only going to see me as a very wise male friend and, too, since she was highly allergic to cats, would never, on that alone, be able to visit me.

I had never been to a museum before in my life and not looked at the pictures, yet not one picture was missed. It was a magical afternoon. If Eloise should ever get married again, I only hope she marries the right man to love her.

CHAPTER THIRTEEN: STAR ("Star_nyc")

LETTERS:

Jejune548

Dear GoGotcha

Dear Littlesun31

Dear Finally555

Dear Shapelyt2beeyours

Dear Kurn44

Dear Gretta

Dear Eve515

Dear Etoile1607

Dear Byenyc

Hi, Idwtfybtway

Dear Star_nyc

STORY: Star ("Star_nyc")

Jejune548:

I believe you.

Egbert

Dear GoGotcha:

Please don't take me the wrong way, but I don't see how you can say you are "Not looking for Sex." With a picture of you stretched out on the sand like a lamb chop with jeans as tight as your skin on, and a shirt so open I don't even have to tilt my head to see halfway down your beautiful boobs, any straight man is going to want to take you straight to bed. Mix that up with your love of beer & barbecue, and it all spells out "great girl for fun time." Mind you, that is not a bad thing, not at all. You do in fact look like, sound like, give off all the vibes that you are friendly, open, bubbly, and incredibly sexy. But, I doubt that with your being surrounded by all the big lugs in your pictures, and the less than letter-perfect profile you've written (which you do need to proofread or get someone to help you with), you're attracting anything close to the kind of men you seem, perhaps, to really be interested in.

Remember, you attract what it looks like you're selling. And if you really want something else, you need, in my honest opinion, to do a pretty major makeover here. If you do want what it looks you're selling, then you are a blessed woman who can certainly choose any creature that crawls up from the bottom of the sea and over to you on the sandy beach you're lying on she wants.

Just being straight up.

Egbert

Dear Littlesun31,

My, my, my you are a little fireball. You've got a very inviting innocent & white dress thing going, but a little sliver of your tummy showing (where a ring, too, is apparently hidden). You are trying to land the big husband-fish, but, clearly, you like going out and getting drunk at night like any wild and young girl. You tell potential men that if they're not ready to commit to you and settle down (which, by the way, you say without their even having ever met you), then to pass on. But are you, my sly little Japanese goddess, really ready to settle down and commit yourself? I'd love to meet you and talk about these and other matters, and gently guide you home by a soft touch to the elbow late, late at night.

Egbert

Dear Finally555:

I have too much depth, intelligence, and intensity for most people to even want to look at. After all, we do live in a country where, unless one is an elite athlete, "elite" is a bad word. That said, even though I think my profile lilts to the dry side, I am anything but. Its tone is too matter-of-fact and lacks the sort of, well, humanity that lets people into the same space. Intellectually, sure, it's right on. Trust me, in person I am much more personable and quite open — or can be.

I like your profile, by the way; it speaks to ideas and reveals a bit about how you actually feel about things; and, too, the very smart understanding that even if I'm nodding my head *yes yes yes* to everything in it (except NPR which I really can't stand!), no checklist affirming commonly held interests or beliefs confirms or determines, as you say, compatibility.

But in my book, based on what I've read of you and my knowledge of myself, I'd bet on our being able to enjoy playing the grown-up version of show-and-tell — which, I guess, means instead of the little, stuffed, fluffy bunny rabbit with the dingling bell in the ear that you're bringing to class, we might be able to show each other what the otherwise gruff poet Charles Bukowski called the bluebird singing always in his heart — and what quiets it, and what has.

Egbert

Dear Shapelyt2beeyours,

Thank you for your kind and complimentary email. I'm afraid I myself, however, am not so keen on my own profile you liked so much anymore! While I was as honest and inclusive as I could be, I think I might come across as either a bit pretentious or more evolved, or both, than I may in fact be. Be that as it may, for good and for bad, it has screened, I think, a lot of people.

You mention Omega in your profile, and I myself did a workshop there some years ago with Lama Surya Das. It was epochal. It was a weeklong Dzogchen meditation workshop and I felt things that I hadn't felt since being a teenager in Tunisia one summer — in other words, freed, liberated, and open.

You sound as though you have a clear and open and at the same time steady spirit yourself, and I'd be open to meeting for coffee if you'd like; we're practically neighbors, just let me know. I happen to be on vacation this week, and if the weather warms up, it's time to rake out the vegetable garden (organic), and prep it for the new season. But, besides that, and on the spur of the moment trips to the city, I'm pretty open. Hope to hear back from you.

Egbert

Dear Kurn44,

Fascinating profile, one of the few that made me think —
and read it through again. I don't think you're cruel at all;
you're just trying to break it down, figure out what kind of
guy is out there, and what are the odds of your bumping
into him. In a nutshell, you definitely have a bias (and I don't
mean this as a judgment, just as a statistic) favoring available women: 10:1, right? I mean, with your insights, and
let's assume they're correct, a decent guy is in a tough situation; after all, divorced men are the "outcasts," and Match
then becomes the dumping ground, the landfill stuffed with
abusive, dirty, alcoholic losers, etc. If the way you see things
is indeed correct, it may help explain some of the trouble I
myself have had here.

There's one comment that I don't get in your profile, the one
about "good men [who] tend to not leave bad marriages."
Why do you imagine this to be so, if it is? It flies in the face,
I think, of the cultural stereotype, you know, of the good du-
tiful woman as mother to her family's children sticking out a
bad marriage for their sake. But this stereotype you up-end.
What possible reason would a good guy stay in a marriage
that doesn't work for him? I know I didn't.

We're obviously too far apart to have anything personal
happen between us, but we could definitely, I think, have a
worthwhile conversation over these things that might shine
a little light on your path and mine.

Egbert

Dear Gretta,

I am truly very sorry to have freaked you out and was aware of my blunders. My "liking you so much" without having met you wasn't about my "having a hole to be filled." Rather, I failed to let you see me just as I am, doubted you would, and threw everything at you to make you "see" me instead. That was the main mistake: forcing you, in effect, to "see" me. I am sorry for making you see me, insisting that you see me the way I did.

Part of my jumping the way I did, however, was also innocent. When I ran across your profile, you immediately struck me as someone worth knowing — someone who was quite the exception to the usual crowd of faces on Match. I leapt out of joy, out of yes, a joyous fantasy, that there was someone here smart, whole, and fascinating — as I see myself as; and when I find others in life like this, I pursue in them sometimes friendship, and sometimes love.

So while I am sorry for how I went about approaching you, I wish that you might also understand that I was just overjoyed over even the possibility of knowing someone really worth knowing. At the root, it's just that simple. My approach to you was still terrible, maladroit, overbearing, and, yes, obsessive; but, it was a knee-jerk response to a feeling of joy. And joy, in my book, is a very good thing.

I am asking you to reconsider, and to get to know me, and me you, little by little; and if it works, great; if not, then not; and to let that take, whichever way it does, however much time it needs to take — and not let my initial blunderbuss ways blow it all away.

I know: I wasn't patient; I let nothing percolate. I am asking you to do both; I will do the same myself. Promise. And we both might find a new friend in each other — and, Lord knows, how precious that really is.

If nothing more is to come of this, I really am sorry, as I said at the beginning, that I freaked you out.

Egbert

Dear Eve515:

How'd a nice girl like you stumble across a weirdo like me? I'm intemperate and grandiose, and poke fun at virtually anything that doesn't strike me as truthful. In fact, I'm so passionate about virtually everything that appeals to me, I blow the very people right out my path whom I'd really like to know and meet. Of course, all you have to do is give me some of that excellent 86% dark Icelandic chocolate, the thick one in the white wrapper at Whole Foods, and I'll play dumb and sweet. Some knucklehead on this site dumped me because she thought my ardent ways (like this) befit one who needed a hole in himself filled. Me, I just think Hamlet needs someone better than Horatio to play ping-pong with, and someone with a little more spunk than whiny Ophelia at checkers or lawn tennis or whatever it was. Do any of these "cancel the other out"? Not in my world; in my world they build it up. So, if you're fun enough, truly and really playful enough, and would really like to hear about what Mr. Frost is really ruing, to which you allude in your profile, and not the usual trite rendition every mediocre teacher hands down like a dead pair of cracked ski boots from the 70's, give me an e-buzz and we'll sling some words back and forth and see how each other's shoes fit.

yours,

Egbert

Dear Etoile1607,

Steven Pinker, whom you've read most recently, writes about Romantic Love in his book from around ten years back called *How the Mind Works*. If that's not the book you know, it'd be worth it just to go to Barnes & Noble and look that section up in the index. It's there. It pretty much sums it up. If you do, please let me know what you think.

Egbert

Dear Byenyc,

I had fun chatting with you.

I wanted to get your name at the end, but you had signed off. Would you?

I'll check in before you fly, but just in case I get caught up and don't, happy travels; fly safe; have a blast.

Egbert

Hi, Idwtfybtway:

The Dalai Lama, whom you mention as your favorite person, I saw just three years ago. He gave a talk, looking over a small green field in which about a thousand of us were seated. The first thing he said, as he pointed to an old graveyard just beside the field, on the other side of an iron fence, was, with a smile, "The final destination!" So be it!

My guess, and it's really only a "look into your eyes" sort of guess, is that you are a joyful and warm person who has never lost her sense of wonder, who knows that this alone is the jewel of life. That, to me, is the freshness that, when I see a giant shadow passing on the ground, I look up again with boylike glee to see a Great Blue Heron flying overhead. At the same time, when I am working with others who are curious, my mind functions with ease and precision, able to hear their ideas and synthesize them with my own in order to, as their leader, create a necessary proposal or plan.

Am I "the one"? Will "your search be over"? Both would be nice of course, a sort of miracle of luck, timing, and belief. Click through my pictures; there's one just of my eyes; look into mine too! I'd be happy to see where it goes.

Best,

Egbert

Dear Star_nyc:

I am "introverted, quirky, smart, kind, and adventurous." I do have, however, a "scary ulterior motive."

If you'd like to find out if I will start by nibbling at your toes first, or the top of your head, please write me back!

Fellow Virgo, and Radiohead lover,

Egbert

Star ("Star_nyc")

From her picture, I thought she'd be hot. I thought she'd be hip. I mean, I knew she was way too young, but I didn't care. I like people who play, and this one, sitting in her little camouflage shorts, half drunk in half her photos, saying how the most recent books she'd read were a bunch of Princeton Review, standardized test study guides for MCATs, GMATs, LSATs, and the like, seemed to have a good sense of humor about Match and the whole thing.

When, pulled over in my car on 14th Street, she texted me from her apartment that she didn't want to come out and meet me as we had planned, after I'd driven hours from upstate New York to meet her at Whole Foods to buy her, as I had promised, the best chocolate bar in the world, I had some trouble breathing. Part of me wanted to yell at her, part of me wanted to help. It was like seeing somebody who's about to jump off a bridge. Yelling at them for being such an asshole for doing such a stupid thing, or reaching out a gentle hand to help them. But my metaphor's a little fucked up because, well, Star felt safe where she was: I was the plunge she was afraid of, into the abyss. I was the unknown.

Texting her back, and then speaking to her from my cellphone in my car, I soothed and comforted her enough. I acknowledged the reasonability of her fears and concerns. I put to the side my own reasons and sense of right and sense of annoyance. They'd be losing arguments if employed, for sure, anyway; and I paid attention to what this poor, scared girl might not have imagined ever really being possible: to go from the virtual, cyberworld hideout of dress-up dreams & desires, to the one of sight & sounds & real smells on dirty Earth's sidewalk.

Unfortunately, once I arrived at Whole Foods as previously planned, she must have seen me look past her and toward another woman standing at the butcher's counter where we had agreed to meet. The overlooking of a woman you have arranged to meet accompanied, too, by the passing but momentary desire for another that will fill a man's eyes, this infinitesimal betrayal, when seen by the one passed over, which it was, is the irrevocable death step of all romance. No amount of wine and shoe polish will ever cover it up. It is fatal, and it lasts forever. I did in fact buy this young woman, who was buttoned up and dressed like Lieutenant Columbo, and never during our date loosened even the belt of her three-quarter length trench coat, the delicious chocolate bar, as promised.

We next had coffee at a Starbucks. She told me about her ten year plan. Her father was a venture capitalist and had a small company. She was going to take it over. She read review books for professional degrees and exams for such on a daily, regular basis. To me, her life was in as orderly shape as a straitjacket. She believed in it wholly. There was no family for herself in it; there was no child in it; there was no husband in it; there was no man in it. It was all about business, and happiness to Star meant being successful at business, which meant taking over her father's company in ten years, for which she was training.

I was torn between going ahead to want to fuck her someday for the helluva it, because it would have been something of a challenge to get there, and because, perversely, I didn't even find her attractive, besides the fact that she was misguided, forlorn, young, and Asian; and not upsetting this little apple cart's life. A guy like me in bed with her, a guy like me in her life would tear her apart. Christ! I could just see myself becoming part of her ten year plan. It was not the place I was going. Nor she. Star thanked me with politeness for the chocolate bar, and shook my hand up to the second knuckles of her fingers when we parted.

CHAPTER FOURTEEN: MARIA ("mariamaria")

LETTERS:

Dear Genevieve

Dear Very Beautiful Woman

Dear Camille22

Hi, Emergencybrake

Hi, Novanova

Hi, VCM20

Honey

Dear Cherieat6608

DEAR STARBRIGHTPHDLLD

Dear Feztram

Dear Amelia

Dear Florenceluvr

Dear mariamaria

STORY: Maria ("mariamaria")

Dear Genevieve,

You are so beautiful you can get anything you want.

Your requests and desires are totally outrageous.

But, as I said:

You are so beautiful you can get anything you want.

Only a child would make requests and desires as outrageous as yours.

But, as you said:

You are to be treated as a goddess.

And, I believe, again:

You are so beautiful you can get anything you want.

Just ask,

Egbert

Dear Very Beautiful Woman:

I do hope you are joking about becoming a housewife. You should not be one. You should be a queen. And, as Queen, you should have servants to do your housework. Me, I will be your most humble tutor. From time to time, I will point out to your Grace's attention, slight errors, which if corrected, will better your appearance before the world at large. For instance, you made a small mistake in your spelling, and might consider changing "Desprerate" to "Desperate." Please accept my attention to this tiny detail as nothing more than a desire to see Your Beauty's perfection reflected in the words you write as well.

Humbly,

Egbert

Dear Camille22:

You look fun, you sound fun, and I bet you are fun. You sound right to the point — after one or two emails, the whole email thing with a stranger that you mention, it really doesn't make any sense, does it? Why do I think you're so fun? That third picture of you — the guys in the background checking you out is great!

Egbert

Hi, Emergencybrake,

You've hit on something I stumbled across a while ago here on Match. Seen as a place to find, or rather, to pursue love, it feels over and over like a cul-de-sac. Then, one stops pursuing that direction. Instead, it is an amazing place to meet people I never would. Period. Next weekend, for instance, I'll be attending an MFA opening at Yale. Whose? A friend I made here. I have made friends with people in California, and have since moved into the other sphere of Facebook — where I've engaged in encouraging a new friend to solve her legal issues. Or, suggested to another woman in New York, that she go to Omega, or just to pick up a copy of Julia Cameron's *The Artist's Way*. No doubt, I've had all sorts of less felicitous meetings as well. People who, during a walk together through Dia in Beacon, could not for the life of themselves give up their Nietzschean battles. Still, other times, I've simply talked to a woman who later became a new friend in the café at MoMA — and we never saw the art. It was beautiful. I have walked through the cherry trees blooming in the Brooklyn Botanic Garden for the first time in 15 years — with someone else new. I have bought a chocolate bar for a sad young woman at Whole Foods. I've had darker moments, too: a Harvard PhD showing up in the middle of the night, having driven for two hours to my house, two weeks in a row, after our brief relationship had been definitely ended, and had to turn her away, door locked, her beating on it. So, it is MOSTLY fun, but not always! And there are people I wish I had met, but have been so over-the-top myself with enthusiasm, that I lost them. I learn from this just as much, but in a different way. I'm happy to have guided one woman to believe that she really had a book to write about her falafel sales while following Phish for three years, and that she didn't have to give up her success-driven lifestyle in New York, and remain true to herself. Strange, wondrous, unexpected, troubling, enlightening things have happened here. Love? Maybe not in the personal, as in one person way; I haven't experienced that here; but, overall there has been a goodness, a kindness, a human sort of usefulness between me and others that I think counts for it as well.

Egbert

Hi, Novanova,

You sound great. Even though we'll never meet, given that New Haven is an uncomfortable 2 1/2 hour jag from where I live, there are plenty of things we both like. Radiohead and Dostoyevsky, for starters. I must say, however, I absolutely hate NPR! So smug and self-serving and really not smart radio at all. I am, I am careless to admit, "wickedly smart and funny." But more even than that and my odd syntax for some reason here right now your simple and to the humble and true point: "Be good company." As Plato writes of Socrates saying while stroking the fine golden curls of Lysis, he would give even all the gold of Darius to have friendship, that thing of which his young charge and his beloved are possessed by so easily. Keep on with your fight!

Egbert

Hi, VCM20,

You're obviously thoughtful and very smart. Who knows, you might be brilliant. But I junked all that myself. It got me nowhere here. Sure, my current profile, it's a historical patchwork culled from a bunch of my Match experiences — when I used to broadcast how exceptional I was, and how I, too, was looking for an exceptional person. But, as I said, I junked all that. I'm going silly and clownish now. Broken up sentences. No more flattering emails from Princeton ABD's telling me, "That last sentence is straight out of Proust." Give me a bucket of fried chicken over that! You have to remember that, like a game of war, whose conclusion is predetermined by the turning of the deck's first card, the outcome of the novels you edit is no less uncertain. But here, just as you say, "It just doesn't work that way."

Egbert

Honey,

It's always the self-proclaimed Christian girls who have the most provocative profiles. Here you are, spoon in mouth, holding a piece of apple pie and a sexy boob shot to every heathen boy out there. You make me want to convert. But, I'm afraid, since you work for your Dad's company, that the wrath of God Himself is not too far away from your Formica kitchen countertop. I swear, I wish I were devout. For a girl as pretty as you, I'd eat your faith and Lord in a heartbeat.

Egbert

Dear Cherieat6608,

I wish to Zeus I had a girlfriend as pretty as you. But, alas, we have like zilch in common. Best of luck!

Egbert

DEAR STARBRIGHTPHDLLD:

OH. MY. GOD.

YOU HAVE SCRATCHED OUT ALL THOSE PEOPLE'S FACES.

THAT IS SO UPSETTING TO SEE.

WHEREAS,

YOU ARE, BY YOUR OWN ADMISSION, "STAR-BRIGHT," I BESEECH YOU: BUY A DIGITAL CAMERA FOR A HUNDRED BUCKS, SET THE AUTO-TIMER, AND TAKE A HANDFUL OF SELF-PORTRAITS. IT'LL SOOTHE THE FEARS OF YOUR LITIGIOUS SOUL THAT THAT CHILD'S GUARDIAN(S) AND YOUR CO-HORTS WILL SUE YOU; AND, GOD-BE-WILLING, EASE YOUR PHILOSOPHICAL SPIRIT OVER THIS ACT OF VIOLENT HUMAN DEFACEMENT.

WHEREAS,

UNLESS YOU'RE MS. RAND HERSELF WHOSE RO-MANTIC PINCERS MOVED IN ON A GUY THREE DECADES HER JUNIOR, IT IS VERY HARD TO IMAGINE YOUR CLAIM TO BEING A "ROMANTIC" AND STILL LIKE THE IDEAS ESPOUSED BY *ATLAS SHRUGGED*. DOESN'T ADD UP.

WHEREAS,

ALTHOUGH I AM A "NICE GUY," I DO NOT EVER WANT TO IMAGINE THE POSSIBILITY OF MY FACE BEING SCRATCHED OFF LIKE A QUIK-PIK LOTTO TICKET BY A LADY WITH FERVOR AT A GAS STA-TION, ANYMORE THAN I WISH TO DREAM ABOUT

IT BEING CHEWED OFF AT NIGHT BY A DOBERMAN
PINSCHER.

EGBERT

Dear Feztram,

I'm sorry, but that part about long, wet kisses going on for three days so grossed me out I just started laughing and had to write you. Eeeew! God help us all with the educated person who's got a handle on the parenthetical, I say! Some kind of weird *sotto voce* thing going on, I guess. But, how the heck would I know? I was never as a child a "little grown-up in training." Isn't that how earlier American portraiture was? Little grown-ups in wooden frames? But how the heck would I know, right? I grew up in Connecticut, where we did not grow up at all: we just got older.

Egbert

Dear Amelia,

Thanks for the note. I'll have you know that I must take exception to your naked man vacuuming. I thought I had the patent on that. Years and years ago I discovered that when cleaning the house, really cleaning it, I got sweaty of course and basically wrecked the clothes I was in. Besides, once sweaty, who likes to take sweaty clothes off first before jumping in showers? Joe Namath, maybe. (that's one of three sports heroes I know.) So, I simply began cleaning house having taken them all off. By the time one is doing the nasty bathroom, one is so mucky and foul, well, you get the point: it doesn't matter anymore. And voilà, when finished, straight into the shower. Why did I always think this was my baby, my invention, my *secretum secretorum*?

Egbert

Dear Florenceluvr:

Nobody "falls for a writer." I've written, and I'm a writer. I've written better than this; you would be stunned at how much I've written. Just here. Every day. It is work. Reading through all these mostly inane profiles. You'd think women had nothing going on except traveling to Machu Picchu and the like. I do not care about where anybody has traveled. To me it's like having your teeth checked. Why even bother telling anyone? You, however, know you have something to say. Yes, you do. You're a born bank robber, a regular Ma Barker. One of the good ones. I do like the bit about what you said "you'd mistake me for." Does this imply you're not "loyal, kind, honest, ethical"? It's only logical, and I am, after all, a reader.

Egbert

Dear mariamaria,

Cap-a-pe, I like everything you say in your profile. You sound alive & fun & creative. But, rather than pace the ramparts, and go on about how this and that I am, which I am, I'll let you take a peek at me through the mist and see what you think.

Egbert

Maria ("mariamaria")

I can't remember if I paid for dinner or not, for both of us, but I do recall picking out filet mignon, against the waitress' suggestion. After all, you can't beat filet mignon, and I knew that. Maria followed my lead. This was after driving around through some strip-hell of New Jersey, two hours south of me, where we'd already ditched one nice enough looking Italian restaurant because of paint smells, exiting beneath the nose of a kind enough gentleman who both understood and wished to protest our sudden and unfortunate leave-taking. I did like that spirit of hers, just to get up and leave; and I liked, too, how for the first half hour, rather than sitting down somewhere over bad coffee, we walked around a sports field and sat in the aluminum bleachers, trading some of the facts of our lives. That she did this in a white dress, and didn't show concern over getting it dirty, was a real plus to me, too.

I had to, as is often the case, push to the side that Maria was less attractive than she appeared online. There, she was a princess. Here, in real life, she was attractive, but would not stop the show. She looked tired and a bit beat down, as did her car, a late 90's Honda she pulled up in next to my Saab. Hell, I know I look a bit beat down myself, so these things I tend to let go of pretty easily. After all, the picture in the menu is supposed to look better than what turns up on your plate. It's advertising, and you'd be a fool, unless you were some untapped Adonis type, to put yourself out there looking like we all do after some forty plus revolutions around the Sun after one more long hard day in the brain box, not to mention a pummeled enough heart.

But there were many things about this woman that threw me off. I did not like her lie in her online profile about not having a child when she did. Sure, I said I was divorced when I was separated, but I was getting divorced. I in no way wished to remain married to my wife. Did I deceive myself that it was merely titular? Yes, I did. But that was about how much pain remaining married to her was still causing me, not some desire or urge or longing to hang onto her. God, no. That was my lie. And I admit now it was a little more than just technical. But a child? How could you do that? How could you deny that? That's not technical. That stone of judgment I did cast silently into the waters while we talked with ease over our beef dinners.

We were enjoying each other's company so much that we stopped in another place and had what I had hoped would be good coffee. It was a huge hacienda-type place with few and silent workers. A bartender made our drinks whose order was taken by another. Maria had the house's specialty which was some sort of coffee concoction with alcohol, like a hot toddy, some ski drink, and I a double espresso. It didn't make her drunk, but it — or being with me — did make her comfortable. And, as I listened to her sad story about being sexually harassed at the local community college's nursing program by a teacher — a lecherous Argentinean male nurse — who'd failed her by her not putting out for him, and how the whole establishment closed in and surrounded her like a bunch of Swiss pikemen, like Myrmidons killing Hector, when she brought it to the administration's attention, I felt worse and worse for Maria.

There was a vulnerability to her which is a good thing, but also brittleness and an anger that pushed me away. There was stuff that didn't add up. She seemed to have no attachment to her own child, not that divorced mothers must be primary caretakers, as the legal lingo of parenthood goes, but the lack of affection I felt from her made this child seem not even what Thomas Hardy derisively calls children of ignorant parents their "appurtenances." Even if I can't care and love children of another myself, the lack of care and love, if I sense this from a parent, anything but feeling joy and love unbridled for one's children, this strikes me deeper than anything else I know on earth. I guess I'm tossing a second stone of judgment where the first one already went.

Maria's exasperation over a man she told me she'd dated who was still buzzing her phone repeatedly while we were out together was a another huge stone in the water. That a) her phone was on to let it happen; and b) that it kept happening; and c) that it'd been going on with him for two weeks like this; and d) that I had to know and hear all about it — these were big stones. It also came out that, at noon, I was Maria's second date of the day. Even though I myself have killed two birds with one stone by having back-to-back dates in White Plains with two women, for instance, hearing about it from Maria so offhandedly was a serious put off. Even if everything's flibbity-jibbity, don't make the one you're with feel that way. This to me is where tact, decorum, and upbringing come into play. Others might argue that that's also where my hypocrisy and deceit rear their consumptive heads, and this might be true, too.

Even though Maria said she wanted to come upstate to see where I lived next time, and I probably agreed with her at the time that that would be nice, she was a woman I'd end up sleeping with a few times, maybe a month or two, and never fall in love with. That's what I saw as plain as day: I wasn't going to fall in love with Maria. I actually could put up with and accept her lying a bit about her personal life and the other stuff. I liked her. She was fun and had some spirit. But I wasn't ever going to fall in love with her. I could recognize that like I could see the Ace of Spades. I could feel that, and let it go without a further care.

CHAPTER FIFTEEN: MICHELLE ("icouldbe347")

LETTERS:

Dear Diamond339

Dear Demetershines

Dear Lori434

Dear Yankeemadedesign

Dear ISONmonkey

Dear "Linda"

Hey wildkitty

Dear Green_cloud_rain

Dear Wgknyc

Dear Ur4now

Dear Izabelle

Dear Adzukibean22

Dear Flaxengirl47

Dear Wholeness

Hi, Katharine

Dear Chantaljlm

Dear Jeralan

Dear Merylist685

Dear icouldbe347

STORY: Michelle ("icouldbe347")

Dear Diamond339:

A real aesthete.

A true beauty.

You dazzle the smart ones,

and cull all the weirdos.

The ill-read and dumb ones,

just delete them.

Delete me,

if you'd like;

You'll probably never

run across another XY

Gödel-Escher type who's

as playful & smarter.

Egbert

Dear Demetershines:

Lord Byron was cocky.

So was Shelley.

Einstein flapped his arms & crowed for five minutes straight when his first paper was published. Does that count too?

Archimedes? Cocky as all hell.

Kafka? You might not think so, but anyone who says,

"I am nothing but literature" is.

Joyce: cocky.

Francis Crick. Very cocky.

Gertrude Stein? Obviously.

"This is my letter to the world"? Emily, too.

I don't think Nietzsche or Pound really were.

Hegel and Wagner. Definitely were.

Descartes? Vain, but not cocky.

Rousseau, in an offhand way.

Wittgenstein? Cockiness doesn't get any better than that.

Goethe, by the way, mentions in his diary about how insecure he felt and how depressed it made him at least once a week or so.

Egbert

Dear Lori434:

The last thing a chick as hot as you are needs to do is take half her clothes off online. But, I confess, I do get a kick out of the cat woman* with a PhD approach. It does take some real chutzpah to do it. So, mazel tov. However, as I'm sure your overstuffed inbox is living proof of, a little Asian herbivore like you is probably attracting only big dumb white carnivores who roam the streets like overstuffed, cholesterol-impeded wolves. If that's the type of animal you want, more power to you; if you want a lithe, nimble, Blake-like Tyger who's as smart as any beast you may ever find prowling the planet with a couple of XY chromosomes, write back, and give my cage a little rattle.

*yes, I know I've mixed the cat and herbivore stuff, but it sounds too good to change it, unless you can think of another sexy vegetarian animal, besides you, of course.

Egbert

Dear Yankeemadedesign:

Nobody respects age range; it's a waste of time. You cannot overcome this; it's also a waste of time. Then, one day, having been caught in the trap of never having been taken as who you are, rather than consistently and constantly being taken as what you are, you discover you are even older than the ceiling you placed long ago, and wonder: Did I make a mistake? These of course are the chances we all take, but few are as likely to be ensnared by the traps fate sets than the beautiful & the lovely, the tender & the kind. Such a one are you.

Egbert

Dear ISONmonkey:

Décolleté on a bridge, stunning on a ladder, I can't figure out where the degree in education comes in. I do, however, unlike you, love bugs. When a spider appears hatched on the bottom of my bathtub in the morning, before it gets swooshed away, I pick it up and drop it out the window slid open. "After all these years," either yours or mine, sure, I know myself pretty damn well. I'll tell you the truth, straight up: I'm a totally outrageous human being, an iconoclast who walks in step like a soldier of utmost conformity; I'm as playful as a baby cougar, and quite fierce at times with incompetent or middling adults; I love being alone; I adore people who twinkle and who are kind. I know how to fall in love with a moment, and to let that moment go if it doesn't come back. I am helpful and caring for the people I care about and love. I am endlessly creative as a writer. Fools, I give short shrift to.

Egbert

Dear "Linda,"

Either your photo is wrong or your age is wrong or you're one of those Russian scammers trying to get some pathetic middle-aged dope to send you money at customs at JFK.

Please let me know which one it is.

Thanks,

Egbert

Hey wildkitty,

I definitely do not have pleats in my pants. Eeew! They're an instant turnoff. I can't even look at a guy who's wearing them. But, I will let you choose which flavor popsicle you want out of the box first.

Egbert

Dear Green_cloud_rain:

Are you left-handed, or just pretending to play guitar?

Egbert

Dear Wgknyc:

Years ago now I went on a camping trip with an ex-girlfriend. I felt guilty reading Kierkegaard, reading about the young girl he jilted in his skewed way of thinking, and slept with her again. She's happily married to a putz who's as bright as a nightlight now. Of course no one ever wants to hear about an ex, especially, I should say, as the first breadcrumbs to tumble out of my fingers. But, you, you are unusually smart and genuinely shameless, the latter a great virtue, the former just being the necessary chips to pull a chair up to the table, and I expect the humor will warm some membranes. I love, by the way, making smart people blush; and it's lovely, in all truth, that someone whose profile is somewhat a tortoise-shell carapace, can. Blushing is lovely; it captures the heart.

Egbert

Dear Ur4now,

You have a very sexy mind; it goes with the pocketbook.

Egbert

Dear Izabelle:

To the extent that you "don't like talking about yourself," I love talking about myself. I'm a born egomaniac. Fortunately, I've learned to curb my voracious appetite to take over and subdue an entire dinner table with my tales and wanton arrogance, with an attentive ear. But, alas, most people would, in the end, prefer to hear my ridiculous yarns and bombast over the grayed-out tales of their own lackluster lives. You don't seem like you're much of a talker at all, really. I can understand that, with your looks and intelligence a sure bet every time. Me, I just went berserk, long ago and far away, with making myself smart. Sure, it got me into some interesting spots in Budapest & Saint Petersburg & Prague, but it never got me home. That was just dumb luck.

Egbert

Dear Adzukibean22,

I love reading your profile; I've done it twice.

Egbert

Dear Flaxengirl47:

I am an emotional vampire, but I will give you all my blood. So, put down that book you're reading, and make sure your top is tied when you sit up.

Egbert

Dear Wholeness,

You are the living portrait of health. You hair glows and your skin radiates. Me, I'm a dirt-under-the-fingernails kind of guy who likes to come inside with a bunch of carrots from the garden and read a little Pascal. Honestly, though, *The Tibetan Book of Dying* is most definitely an important read. At times there is nothing to do but sit. Nothing to do, real Beckett-like. I'm afraid, though, my sense of the spiritual is pretty grounded here on earth, like giving people the correct change back, in a metaphorical way of being. Lama's often dig me, stop in their footsteps and have admired the lines of my forehead. I just go on and get a cup of coffee, after nodding, and ask the girl behind the register if she's having a good day, and get on with my business.

Egbert

Hi, Katharine:

I grew up in Connecticut, too. It was the worst experience of my life, but I am grateful for it all. That which we are, we are, as old Tennyson said, right? Peace, sister.

Egbert

Dear Chantaljlm:

Only when I see women like you do I question the wisdom of my having moved away from Greenwich.

Egbert

Dear Jeralan,

No, I'm afraid for me, it's the latter. None of it adds up. Why? While I'm not expecting some post angst-ridden manifesto for a profile, I still get a little bit puzzled over how smart, Ivy League-educated people, people who have gone through such a thorough round of exposure (and in some cases double exposure) to the best thinking and top-notch minds around, can still be such chatterboxes! All I hear is good grammar. But, maybe I've got it all wrong: you could simply be an absolutely delightful person who hasn't been crushed by the overweening excesses and privileges of the Northeast. Maybe you're just comfortable and happy with yourself, and really have nothing to prove. Could it be nothing more than you're just a good person who was intelligent enough and lucky enough to go after and get a great education? By George, I think I've got it! Mazel tov.

Egbert

Dear Merylist685:

The facts that you just finished Tolstoy, are an editor and a writer, and describe yourself as "not run of the mill" are certainly draws; no doubt, in person, lest you think otherwise, I do not speak in any way that resembles these words here, however easy they are for me to plunk down so: I am only having fun, and appealing, or at any rate, attempting to appeal, to your stated liking for a well-turned sentence, or somesuch utterance. In truth, I am incredibly playful, self-aware, and, like the great forlorn aristocrat Levin, flawed in all the right places.

Egbert

Dear icouldbe347,

Every now and then I run across someone who genuinely sounds happy with herself, who is grateful, as you say about waking up each morning for the way things are. It is so refreshing for me to hear this. I'll have to admit, though, that I've gotten a little bit jaded here on this site — against what seems to be an endless barrage of exotic travel destinations and enough cultural activities listed to sink a medium-sized ocean liner. They never impress me, and sound more like dreams or symbols or proofs of having a "meaningful" life. And while it is true that in the past I lived in faraway places, today I was planting arugula seeds, beans, bok choy seeds, mustard green seeds, and others in my garden, something quiet and simple that I love to do.

As you work in health and wellness and carry that awareness into all aspects of your life, and say, quite rightly, that our careers "undoubtedly impact our personal lives as well," my job, which I do with passion and energy and near madness at times, for which I am revered and deeply rewarded in many ways, definitely carries over — not the work itself, but the spirit of it into the rest of my life. Or, maybe it's my life as a writer, outside of my job, that carries into that. At any rate!!!!

It was a real pleasure to read someone's profile who looks and sounds like she's got it all going right.

Egbert

Michelle ("icouldbe347")

When I stopped at the corner of East 85th Street and 2nd Ave, I could not believe my good fortune. There, standing across the street waiting for me, was a woman so sweet I could hardly believe my eyes. With my wicker picnic basket in one hand, the two of us took off walking towards Central Park where I had proposed we go; and the whole while we walked, I kept catching glimpses of this beautiful woman who kept turning her head to look at me, her smile beaming.

Dressed in an orange cotton dress, Michelle had a smile that was the catch of everyone's eye, and for the entire brisk walk, I felt I was the catch of hers. I laid the blanket down at a spot she had chosen close to the trees at the west side of the park, and amidst cheese and crackers and all sorts of goodies I had brought, we talked like butterflies. I began to feel ill when she told me about the collapse of her most recent relationship, about a man who had filed but not completed his divorce, about how, in the end, in spite of her love for him, his residual feeling for his to-be ex-wife destroyed the relationship Michelle had had with him. When I saw how badly she had been hurt by this, I had to tell her that while I had posted that I was divorced on my profile, I was only separated. I realized that for this woman, I had to be straight up, right then and there. And while I told her the truth about my marital situation, that I was in the process of getting divorced, I wept because I was so afraid that Michelle would just get up from the blanket and walk away.

Later that evening as I walked her to her apartment and bade her goodbye, I asked her at her front stoop, "What is a gentleman supposed to do? Kiss you goodnight or not?" She smiled, I kissed her on her cheek, and drove two hours home north.

With Michelle, I felt hot, young, and sexy. We would ride the subway together and people would stare at us. I would whisper in her ear, "They just don't understand. They are asking themselves: 'What is this hot black girl doing with this white skinhead?'" And we would not mind them a bit; no, it was flattering.

Both of us in our forties, we would go to Central Park where we had first met, with snacks and a Frisbee. We were the stars of the park. We could throw the Frisbee so far, so straight, that people would come up to me and ask me for advice. Men would watch Michelle throw the disc and both of us reveled. It was summer, it was hot; I was lean, and I was fit. I tossed the Frisbee with my shoes and shirt off. My body was a thing of speed, accuracy, grace, and power. And Michelle's, well, women would stop her in the street and just say to her, "You have an amazing body." We both smiled. Their attention just reflected our physical sexiness, which I felt I was borrowing, in part, from Michelle whose 5'3" body was toned like a sculpture.

I was just as happy when Michelle came to visit me upstate. She would hop off the bus, sometimes disconsolate if I was five minutes late at the bus station, and the next morning we would play tennis on the town courts. Or, we would play late in the afternoon until the sun went down. And except for her habit of chatting with a blithe sort of regularity about ex-boyfriends at just about anytime, which irked me as bizarre, I loved the fun we were having together.

Smoking pot and eating vegetarian food became a regular thing with Michelle. I hadn't smoked pot in a good sixteen years. It was fun. Unfortunately, our minds went in two different directions when we got high. My mind would begin telling stories, writing poems, and thinking; hers would want us to relate to each other, to share the high together. But it wasn't anything I could do anything about. Even around sex, when I got high, I was as good as an explorer remembering his journeys to Antarctica. Having prided herself on her vibrant sexuality, this frustrated her.

My entire being as a writer and my entire trove of writing was left out of this relationship. It felt good. I felt liked and accepted for just being who I was: a guy. I had never been somebody's "guy"; being called her "guy," that made me feel super-attractive. Yeah, to be someone who was sporty, and hip, who went to cool concerts in Williamsburg, this was something I just hadn't really been or done or been known by. It was a new side. And not to feel any pressure to be some intellectual/genius writer, man, I really got along with that. It was cool having a hot chick who just had the sweets for me, and, as for my subscription to Match, I'd just let it run out without another thought, like it was nothing.

Michelle's ambitions to be a songwriter I was totally behind and did my best to teach her how to read music. She would play the same bars on my piano over and over, and sing the same verses over and over. I went to B&H with her where she bought an electric piano for her apartment in the city. But, the quiet backdrop of this was her huge disappointment over her last relationship before me with a very talented guitarist with whom together she had cut several tracks of her original songs and covers of other artists. She was very frustrated about how to really get her music going. There was only so much I could do here.

After seven or eight months of alternating trips to the city or the country, Michelle told me she wanted me to sit down one evening. I sat down. "How long do you think this can go on like this?" she asked. To me, this question meant: When are we going to move in together, or talk about moving in together, or get married? These questions all meant the same exact thing to me: the future. I had had no such thoughts of these things. I was happy the way things were. But I understood in an instant that Michelle was going somewhere else with this that I had not imagined. I had been in the moment for eight months, and she all of a sudden was not.

She had been at several times during the relationship concerned about how we talked with each other on the phone when we were apart. While I understood what she meant, there was nothing I could do to be more affectionate or connected with her during the week that way. The relationship was so grounded in sports, sex, and smoking pot that I wasn't sure what I might have talked about with her on the phone. My writing? That wasn't going to happen. I simply enjoyed being with her when I was.

I wrote her an email explaining that I liked the way things were, and that I actually did not want things to encroach on my feeling free which I felt having to talk to Michelle every night (and failing to satisfy her) did. I drove down to the city the next weekend to give back some of her things that were at my house, and to receive from her some of my things that were at her apartment, and to say in person, goodbye.

I don't know if I've ever seen anyone so heartbroken in my life. She really cared about me, there was no deny. And as fun and sexy as she was, my future was not with her. That had been unexpectedly brought to my attention in a flash the weekend prior. I had to say goodbye.

I looked her up out of curiosity on Facebook about a year later to see if she was there and saw that she had married the guy she'd dated before me. I am totally happy for her: she got exactly what she wanted and deserved. She remains one of the most joyful people I have had the grace to know for a brief while in my life.

www.ingramcontent.com/pod-product-compliance
Lightning Source LLC
Chambersburg PA
CBHW032102280326
41933CB00009B/738